A map of misreading

A map of misreading

Harold Bloom

OXFORD UNIVERSITY PRESS
Oxford   New York   Toronto   Melbourne

Oxford University Press
Oxford   London   Glasgow
New York   Toronto   Melbourne   Wellington
Nairobi   Dar es Salaam   Cape Town
Kuala Lumpur   Singapore   Jakarta   Hong Kong   Tokyo
Delhi   Bombay   Calcutta   Madras   Karachi

Library of Congress Cataloging in Publication Data

Bloom, Harold.
     A map of misreading.
     1. English poetry—Explication.   2. American
poetry—Explication.   3. Poetry.   I. Title.
[PR504.B56 1980]   821'.009   80-15267
ISBN 0-19-502809-0 (pbk.)

Printed in the United States of America
printing, last digit: 10 9 8

For Paul de Man

Acknowledgments

I am grateful for comments and aid from the following friends, without whom I could not have written this antithetical completion to my earlier study of poetic influence: Geoffrey Hartman, J. Hillis Miller, Paul de Man, John Hollander, Angus Fletcher, A. Bartlett Giamatti, James Raimes, and Stephanie Golden.

Contents

As wine in a jar, if it is to keep, so is the Torah, contained within the outer garment. Such a garment is constituted of many stories; but we, we are required to pierce the garment.

Zohar III, 152a

Viewing his Sixfold Emanation scatter'd thro' the deep
In torment . . .

Blake, Milton I, 2, 119–20

A map of misreading

Introduction: a meditation upon misreading

This book offers instruction in the practical criticism of poetry, in how to read a poem, on the basis of the theory of poetry set forth in my earlier book, *The Anxiety of Influence*. Reading, as my title indicates, is a belated and all-but-impossible act, and if strong is always a misreading. Literary meaning tends to become more under-determined even as literary language becomes more over-determined. Criticism may not always be an act of judging, but it is always an act of deciding, and what it tries to decide is meaning.

Like my earlier book, A *Map of Misreading* studies poetic influence, by which I continue *not* to mean the passing-on of images and ideas from earlier to later poets. Influence, as I conceive it, means that there are *no* texts, but only relationships *between* texts. These relationships depend upon a critical act, a misreading or misprision, that one poet performs upon another, and that does not differ in kind from the necessary critical acts performed by every strong reader upon every text he encounters. The influence-relation governs reading as it governs writing, and reading is therefore a mis-writing just as writing is a misreading. As literary history lengthens, all poetry necessarily becomes verse-criticism, just as all criticism becomes prose-poetry.

The strong reader, whose readings will matter to others as well as to himself, is thus placed in the dilemmas of the revisionist, who wishes to find his own original relation to truth, whether in texts or in reality (which he treats as texts anyway), but also wishes to open received texts to his own sufferings, or what he wants to call the sufferings of history. This book, as a study of creative misreading or the belatedness of poetic reading, is also a prolegomenon to further studies of revisionism, and to the ambivalences of canon-formation that rise from revisionism.

What is revisionism? As the origins of the word indicate, it is a re-aiming or a looking-over-again, leading to a re-esteeming or a re-estimating. We can venture the formula: the revisionist strives to *see* again, so as to *esteem* and *estimate* differently, so as then to *aim* "correctively." In the dialectical terms that I will employ for interpreting poems in this book, re-seeing is a *limitation*, re-estimating is a *substitution*, and re-aiming is a *representation*. I displace these terms from the context of later or Lurianic Kabbalism, which I take as the ultimate model for Western revisionism from the Renaissance to the present, and which I intend to study in another book.

Kabbalah, which means "the given," is a particular tradition of images, parables, and quasi-concepts relating to God. Its principal twentieth-century scholar, Gershom Scholem, regards it as a variety of "mysticism," and certainly it has mixed with and fostered a myriad who have experienced extraordinary states of consciousness. But Scholem's own descriptions of Kabbalah emphasize its work of *interpretation*, of revisionary replacements of Scriptural meaning by techniques of *opening*. All Kabbalistic texts are interpretative, however wildly speculative, and what they interpret is a central text that perpetually possesses authority, priority, and strength, or that indeed can be regarded as *text itself*. *Zohar*, most influential of Kabbalistic books, is the true forerunner of Post-Enlightenment strong poetry, not in its grotesque content or its formless forms, but in its *stance towards the precursor text*, its revisionary genius and mastery of the perverse necessities of misprision. The psychology of belatedness, which Freud partly developed but partly concealed or evaded, is the invention of Kabbalah, and Kabbalah remains the largest single source for material that will help us to study the revisionary impulse and to formulate techniques for the practice of an antithetical criticism.

Isaac Luria, sixteenth-century master of theosophical speculation, formulated a regressive theory of creation, in a revision of the earlier Kabbalistic emanative theory of creation. The Lurianic dialectic of creation has been studied illuminatingly by Scholem, particularly in his recent book *Kabbalah*, and the reader is referred to it as background for the theoretical parts of my book. But all that is strictly necessary for my purposes here are a few remarks on Luria's system.

The Lurianic story of creation now seems to me the best paradigm available for a study of the way poets war against one another in the strife of Eternity that is poetic influence. Luria's story, in whatever version, has three main stages: *Zimzum, Shevirath hakelim, Tikkun. Zimzum* is the Creator's withdrawal or contraction so as to make possible a creation that is not himself. *Shevirath hakelim* is the breaking-apart-of-the-vessels, a vision of creation-as-catastrophe. *Tikkun* is restitution or restoration—man's contribution to God's work. The first two stages can be approximated in many of the theorists of deconstruction, from Nietzsche and Freud to all our contemporary interpreters who make of the reading subject either what Nietzsche cheerfully called "at most a rendezvous of persons," or what I myself would call a new mythic being—clearly implied by Paul de Man in particular—the reader as Overman, the *Überleser.* This fictive reader simultaneously somehow negatively fulfills and yet exuberantly transcends self, much as Zarathustra so contradictorily performed. Such a reader, at once blind and transparent with light, self-deconstructed yet fully knowing the pain of his separation both from text and from nature, doubtless will be more than equal to the revisionary labors of contraction and destruction, but hardly to the antithetical restoration that increasingly becomes part of the burden and function of whatever valid poetry we have left or may yet receive.

The closest aesthetic equivalent to Lurianic contraction is *limita-*

tion, in the sense that certain images limit meaning more than they restore or represent meaning. Breaking-apart-of-the-vessels is like the aesthetic breaking-apart and replacing of one form by another, which imagistically is a process of *substitution. Tikkun,* the Lurianic restitution, is already almost a synonym for *representation* itself.

The first five chapters of this book are devoted to the theory and techniques of misprision or strong "misreading." The last six chapters are given to interpretative instances: poems by Milton, Wordsworth, Shelley, Keats, Tennyson, Browning, Whitman, Dickinson, Stevens, Warren, Ammons, Ashbery. In the first half, a voyage back to literary origins is made, in quest of a map of misreading. From the intimate alliance between poetic origins and poetic final phases, the voyage goes back first to the process of how literary tradition is formed, next to the sources of that process in a Primal Scene of Instruction, and finally to a meditation on belatedness. This meditation centers on influence as a sixfold, defensive trope for the act of reading/misreading. The relation of tropes, defenses, images, and revisionary ratios is then worked out in a chapter that accompanies the map of misprision, goal of this critical quest. A full-scale reading of one poem, Browning's *Childe Roland to the Dark Tower Came,* then illustrates the use of the map. The map is our guide, in the last section of the book, through many versions of influence, from Milton to the present day.

This final section begins with an analysis of Miltonic allusion, in regard to the trope of metalepsis or transumption, the classical equivalent of the final revisionary ratio that Isaac Luria called *gilgul,* the reincarnation of a precursor through his descendants' acts of lifting up and redeeming the saving sparks of his being from the evil shells or broken vessels of catastrophe. A chapter on Milton's descendants from Wordsworth to Tennyson follows, after which the remainder of the book deals with American poets, starting with the prose seer and poetic theorist Emerson, whose relation to subsequent American poets is parallel to Milton's relation to British poets after him.

Part I
CHARTING THE TERRITORY

I

Poetic origins and final phases

Strong poets are infrequent; our own century, in my judgment, shows only Hardy and Stevens writing in English. Great poets— even Yeats and Lawrence, even Frost—may fail of continuous strength, and major innovators—even Pound and Williams—may never touch strength at all. Browning, Whitman, Dickinson are strong, as are the High Romantics, and Milton may be taken as the apotheosis of strength. Poetic strength comes only from a triumphant wrestling with the greatest of the dead, and from an even more triumphant solipsism. Enormous gifts, the endowment of a Coleridge, or of a lesser but still considerable talent like Eliot, do not avail where strength is evaded, or never attained. Poetic strength, in this sense, rises only from a particular kind of catastrophe—as ordinary consciousnesses must regard the terrible incarnation that can lead to a poet like the very old Hardy or the very old Stevens. This chapter will move from the primal catastrophe of poetic incarnation on to a description of the relation of poetic strength to poetic influence, and then to the final phases of Hardy and Stevens.

I rely in this discussion upon the theory of poetry, Vichian and Emersonian in origin, that I have expounded recently in *The Anxiety of Influence*. The theory, deliberately an attempt at de-idealizing, has encountered considerable resistance during my presentation of it in a number of lectures at various universities, but whether the theory is correct or not may be irrelevant to its usefulness for practical criticism, which I think can be demonstrated. I take the resistance shown to the theory by many poets, in particular, to be likely evidence for its validity, for poets rightly idealize their activity; and all poets, weak and strong, agree in denying any share in the anxiety of influence. More than ever, contemporary poets insist that they are telling the truth in their work, and more than ever they tell continuous lies, particularly about their relations to one another, and most consistently about their relations to their precursors. One of the functions of criticism, as I understand it, is to make a good poet's work even more difficult for him to perform, since only the overcoming of genuine difficulties can result in poems wholly adequate to an age consciously as late as our own. All that a critic, as critic, can give poets is the deadly encouragement that never ceases to remind them of how heavy their inheritance is.

Catastrophe, as Freud and Ferenczi viewed it, seems to me the central element in poetic incarnation, in the fearsome process by which a person is re-born as a poet. Perhaps I should say catastrophe as Empedocles viewed it, for the dualistic vision of Empedocles is the necessary start of any valid theory of poetic origins; but then Empedocles was Freud's acknowledged ultimate precursor, even as Schopenhauer was a closer and rather less acknowledged precursor. The dialectic of cosmic love and hate governs poetic incarnation: "At one time they are all brought together into one order by Love; at another, they are carried each in different directions by the repulsion of Strife." Initial love for the precursor's poetry is transformed rapidly enough into revisionary strife, without which individuation is not possible. Strife, Empedocles held, caused the initial catastrophe, separating out the elements and bringing the Promethean fire of consciousness into being. Poetry is identical neither with a particular mode of consciousness nor with a particular instinct, yet its birth in an individual is analogous to the Empedoclean catastrophe of consciousness and the Freudian catastrophe of instinctual genesis. Empedocles and Freud alike are theorists of *influence*, of the giving that famishes the taker. We move from ocean to land by a drying-up of the oceanic sense, and we learn sublimation through our preconscious memories of a glacial catastrophe. It follows that our most valued activities are regressive. The great Ferenczi, more fecund than Freud or Empedocles at envisioning catastrophes, almost as fecund as Blake, rather frighteningly saw all sexual love as regression, a drive back to ocean. Poetry, perhaps unlike sexual intercourse, most certainly is regressive, as Peacock so charmingly saw. I turn therefore to some surmises upon the catastrophe of poetic incarnation. How are true poets born? Or better, as the Age of Sensibility liked to ask, what makes possible the incarnation of the Poetical Character?

Desiccation combined with an unusually strong oceanic sense is the highly dualistic yet not at all paradoxical answer. Here we can cite the most truly poetic of all true, strong poets, P. B. Shelley, whom it is no longer quite so fashionable to malign, a welcome change from the days of my youth. I will summarize the dedicatory stanzas to *The Revolt of Islam*, stanzas as much one of Whitman's starting-points as one of Yeats's, and stanzas highly relevant to those similarly Shelley-obsessed poets, Hardy, who owed Shelley so many of his ecstatic breakthroughs, and Stevens, who owed Shelley his fiction of the leaves, and of the wind, and of most other movements of the spirit. There is no fuller vision of poetic incarnation in the language, not in Collins, Coleridge, Blake, Keats, not even in *Out of the Cradle Endlessly Rocking*, for Shelley was at once a major skeptical intellect and a unique master of the heart's impulses, and he turned both these forces to the study of poetic origins, seeking there the daemonic ground of his own incurable and involuntary dualism. Stevens, however one loves him, hardly compares well with Shelley on this frightening ground, for he lacked both Shelley's intellectual penetration and Shelley's astonishing *speed* of perception, a speed crucial in the dark realms of origins.

At a particular hour, Shelley says, his spirit's sleep was burst, when he found himself weeping, he knew not why, as he walked forth upon the glittering grass, on a May dawn. But this hour, though it turned quickly from tears to a sense of power, of a sublime hope, was followed rapidly by "A sense of loneliness, a thirst with which I pined." To repair this desiccation, the young poet set forth upon erotic quests, all of which failed him, until he encountered his true epipsyche, Mary Wollstonecraft Godwin, whereupon the spirit of solitude left him. He tries to end in the sense of "a serener hour," yet this hope seems vain, for "I am worn away,/And Death and Love are yet contending for Their prey." The Dedication's climax anticipates the close of *Adonais* some four turbulent years later, for the last vision of Shelley and Mary shows them:

> Like lamps into the world's tempestuous night,—
> Two tranquil stars, while clouds are passing by
> Which wrap them from the foundering seaman's sight,
> That burn from year to year with unextinguished light.

Poetic incarnation results from poetic influence, here the influence of Wordsworth, particularly of his Great Ode, *Intimations of Immortality*. No poet, I amend that to no strong poet, can choose his precursor, any more than any person can choose his father. The *Intimations* Ode chose Shelley, as Shelley's *To a Skylark* chose Hardy, the way starlight flows where it flows, gratuitously. Whether we can be found by what is not already somehow ourselves has been doubted from Heracleitus through Emerson to Freud, but the daemon is not our destiny until we yield to his finding us out. Poetic influence, in its first phase, is not to be distinguished from love, though it will shade soon enough into revisionary strife. "*Protection against* stimuli is an almost more important function for the living organism than *reception of* stimuli" is a fine reminder in *Beyond the Pleasure Principle,* a book whose true subject is influence. Poets tend to think of themselves as stars because their deepest desire is to be an influence, rather than to be influenced, but even in the strongest, whose desire is accomplished, the anxiety of having been formed by influence still persists.

Shelley understood that the *Intimations* Ode, and *its* precursor, *Lycidas*, took divination as their true subject, for the goal of divination is to attain a power that frees one from all influence, but particularly from the influence of an expected death, or necessity for dying. Divination, in this sense, is both a rage and a program, offering desperate intimations of immortality through a proleptic magic that would evade every danger, including nature itself. Take the darkest of Freudian formulae, that "the aim of all life is death," reliant on the belief that "inanimate things existed before living ones." Oppose to it the inherent belief of all strong poets, that the animate always had priority, and that death is only a failure in imagination. Say then that in the process of poetic incarnation the ephebe or new poet, through love, experiences an influx of an antithetical power, antithetical both to the entropy that is nature's and to the unacceptable sublimity of Ananke, goddess who turns the spindle of the Freudian instinctual drive back to the inanimate. All poetic odes of incarnation are therefore Immortality odes, and all of them rely upon a curious divinity that the ephebe has imparted successfully, not to himself, but to the precursor. In making the precursor a god, the ephebe already has begun a movement away from him, a primary revision that imputes error to the father, a sudden inclination or swerve away from obligation; for even in the context of incarnation, of becoming a poet, obligation shines clear as a little death, premonitory of the greater fall down to the inanimate.

Poets tend to incarnate by the side of ocean, at least in vision, if inland far they be. Or if some blocking agent excludes any glimpse of that immortal sea, various surrogates readily enough are found. Poets whose sexual natures manifest unusual complexity—Byron, Beddoes, Darley, Whitman, Swinburne, Hart Crane, among so many others—rarely get very far away from the ocean of incarnation. Poets of more primary sexuality avoid this overt obsession, generally following the Wordsworthian pattern, in which a haunting noise of waters echoes every imaginative crisis. Here we need to brood on the full context of poetic incarnation, remembering that every strong poet in Western tradition is a kind of Jonah or renegade prophet.

Jonah, the aggrieved one, whose name means "dove," descends into the ship, and every such ship "was like to be broken." When he descends from ship into the sea, "the sea ceased from its raging." "I leaped headlong into the Sea," Keats said, to learn there "the Soundings, the quicksands, and the rocks." The Sea:

> . . . with its mighty swell
> Gluts twice ten thousand caverns, till the spell
> Of Hecate leaves them their old shadowy sound.

Jonah, in flight from open vision, was swallowed up and closed in darkness. When the sirocco blew upon the rescued prophet, he wished again for darkness, and the author of his book, giving God the last word, never tells us whether Jonah returned to his vocation. Call Jonah the model of the poet who fails of strength, and who wishes to return to the Waters of Night, the Swamp of Tears, where he began, before the catastrophe of vocation. It is only later, awash in the Word, that the poet questing for strength can sing, with Thoreau:

> Now chiefly is my natal hour,
> And only now my prime of life;
> Of manhood's strength it is the flower,
> 'Tis peace's end, and war's beginning strife.

This does not sound, in its first hush, like a strife's beginning, as here in Whitman:

> The yellow half-moon enlarged, sagging down, drooping, the face
>   of the sea almost touching,

> The boy ecstatic, with his bare feet the waves, with his hair the
>   atmosphere dallying,
> The love in the heart long pent, now loose, now at last tumul-
>   tuously bursting. . . .

The dallying hair is the young Apollo's, and every ephebe is a
new Phoebus, looking to name what cannot be named, finding it
again as mysteriously as Ammons does here, in a long-dead hunch-
back playmate of remote childhood:

> So I said I am Ezra
> and the wind whipped my throat
> gaming for the sounds of my voice
>   I listened to the wind
> go over my head and up into the night
> Turning to the sea I said
>   I am Ezra
> but there were no echoes from the waves. . . .

Poetic origins: the Incarnation of the Poetic Character, if an in-
land matter, takes place near caverns and rivulets, replete with min-
gled measures and soft murmurs, promises of an improved infancy
when one hears the sea again. Just when the promises were be-
trayed, the Strong Poet himself will never know, for his strength
(as poet) is never to suffer such knowing. No Strong Poet can
deign to be a good reader of his own works. The Strong Poet is
strong by virtue of and in proportion to his *thrownness;* having
been thrown farther, his consciousness of such primal outrage is
greater. This consciousness informs his more intense awareness of
the precursors, for he knows how far our being can be thrown, out
and down, as lesser poets cannot know.

Ocean, the matter of Night, the original Lilith or "feast that
famished," mothers what is antithetical to her, the makers who fear
(rightly) to accept her and never cease to move towards her. If not
to have conceived oneself is a burden, so for the strong poet there
is also the more hidden burden: not to have brought onself forth,

not to be a god breaking one's own vessels, but to be awash in the Word not quite one's own. And so many greatly surrender, as Swinburne did:

> A land that is thirstier than ruin;
>   A sea that is hungrier than death;
> Heaped hills that a tree never grew in;
>   Wide sands where the wave draws breath;
> All solace is here for the spirit
>   That ever forever may be
> For the soul of thy son to inherit,
>   My mother, my sea.

Even the strongest, who surrender only at the end, brood too deep upon this beauty, as Shelley brooded: "The sea was so translucent that you could see the caverns clothed with the glaucous sea-moss and the leaves and branches of those delicate weeds that pave the bottom of the water." Their epigoni drown too soon, as Beddoes drowned:

> Come follow us, and smile as we;
>   We sail to the rock in the ancient waves,
> Where the snow falls by thousands into the sea,
>   And the drowned and the shipwrecked have happy graves.

The sea of poetry, of poems already written, is no redemption for the Strong Poet. Only a poet already slain under the shadow of the Covering Cherub's wings can deceive himself this profoundly, with Auden:

> Restored! Returned! The lost are borne
> On seas of shipwreck home at last:
> See! In the fire of praising burns
>   The dry dumb past, and we
> The life-day long shall part no more.

To know that we are object as well as subject of the quest is not poetic knowledge, but rather the knowledge of defeat, a knowledge fit for the pragmaticists of communication, not for that handful who hope to fathom (if not to master) the wealth of ocean, the ancestry of voice. Who could set forth on the poet's long journey, upon the path of laboring Heracles, if he knew that at last he must wrestle with the dead? Wrestling Jacob could triumph, because his Adversary was the Everliving, but even the strongest poets must grapple with phantoms. The strength of these phantoms—which is their beauty—increases as the struggling poet's distance from them lengthens in time. Homer, a greater poet in the Enlightenment than he was even among the Hellenes, is greater yet now in our Post-Enlightenment. The splendors of the firmament of time blaze with a greater fury even as time seems to droop in its decay.

How (even with all hindsight) can we know the true ephebe, the potentially strong poet, from the mass of ocean's nurslings around him? By hearing in his first voices what is most central in the precursors' voices, rendered with a directness, clarity, even a sweetness that they do not often give to us. For the revisionary ratios that will be employed as means-of-defense by the maturing poet do not manifest themselves in the ephebe. They appear only when he quests for fire, when he seeks to burn through every context that the precursors created or themselves accepted. What we see in the ephebe is the incarnation of the poetical character, the second birth into supposed imagination that fails to displace the first birth into nature, but fails only because desire fails when confronted by so antithetical a quest, fiercer than the human can bear to undergo.

Why invoke a process that merely begins poets, as prelude to a consideration of the last phases of Hardy and Stevens? Because poets, as poets, and particularly the strongest poets, return to origins at the end, or whenever they sense the imminence of the end. Critics may be wary of origins, or consign them disdainfully to those carrion-eaters of scholarship, the source hunters, but the poet-in-a-poet is as desperately obsessed with poetic origins, generally despite himself, as the person-in-a-person at last becomes obsessed with personal origins. Emerson, most undervalued (in our time) of American moral psychologists, is acutely aware of the mind's catastrophic growth into full self-awareness:

> It is very unhappy, but too late to be helped, the discovery we have made that we exist. That discovery is called the Fall of Man. Ever afterwards we suspect our instruments. We have learned that we do not see directly, but mediately, and that we have no means of correcting these colored and distorting lenses which we are, or of computing the amount of their errors. . . .

When the strong poet learns that he does not see directly, but mediately through the precursor (frequently a composite figure), he is less able than Emerson to accept a helplessness at correcting the eye of the self, or at computing the angle of vision that is also an angle of fall, a blindness of error. Nothing is less generous than the poetic self when it wrestles for its own survival. Here the Emersonian formula of Compensation is demonstrated: "Nothing is got for nothing." If we have been ravished by a poem, it will cost us our own poem. If the poetic self in us loves another, it loves itself in the other; but if it is loved, and accepts love, then it loves itself less, because it knows itself less worthy of self-love. Poets-as-poets are not lovable and critics have been slow to know this, which is why criticism has not yet turned to its rightful function: the study of the problematics of loss.

Let me reduce my argument to the hopelessly simplistic; poems, I am saying, are neither about "subjects" nor about "themselves." They are necessarily about *other poems*; a poem is a response to a poem, as a poet is a response to a poet, or a person to his parent. Trying to write a poem takes the poet back to the origins of what a poem *first was for him,* and so takes the poet back beyond the pleasure principle to the decisive initial encounter and response that began him. We do not think of W. C. Williams as a Keatsian poet, yet he *began and ended as one,* and his late celebration of his

Greeny Flower is another response to Keats's odes. *Only a poet challenges a poet as poet,* and so only a poet makes a poet. To the poet-in-a-poet, a poem is always *the other man,* the precursor, and so a poem is always a person, always the father of one's Second Birth. To live, the poet must *misinterpret* the father, by the crucial act of misprision, which is the re-writing of the father.

But who, what is the poetic father? The voice of the other, of the *daimon,* is always speaking in one; the voice that cannot die because already it has survived death—*the dead poet lives in one.* In the last phase of strong poets, they attempt to join the undying *by living in the dead poets* who are already alive in them. This late Return of the Dead recalls us, as readers, to a recognition of the original motive for the catastrophe of poetic incarnation. Vico, who identified the origins of poetry with the impulse towards divination (to foretell, but also to become a god by foretelling), implicitly understood (as did Emerson, and Wordsworth) that a poem is written to escape dying. Literally, poems are refusals of mortality. Every poem therefore has two makers: the precursor, and the ephebe's rejected mortality.

A poet, I argue in consequence, is not so much a man speaking to men as a man rebelling against being spoken to by a dead man (the precursor) outrageously more alive than himself. A poet dare not regard himself as being *late,* yet cannot accept a substitute for the first vision he reflectively judges to have been his precursor's also. Perhaps this is why the poet-in-a-poet *cannot marry,* whatever the person-in-a-poet chooses to have done.

Poetic influence, in the sense I give to it, has almost nothing to do with the verbal resemblances between one poet and another. Hardy, on the surface, scarcely resembles Shelley, his prime precursor, but then Browning, who resembles Shelley even less, was yet more fully Shelley's ephebe than even Hardy was. The same observation can be made of Swinburne and of Yeats in relation to Shelley. What Blake called the Spiritual Form, at once the aboriginal poetical self and the True Subject, is what the ephebe is so dangerously obliged to the precursor for even possessing. Poets need not *look* like their fathers, and the anxiety of influence more frequently than not is quite distinct from the anxiety of style. Since poetic influence is necessarily misprision, a taking or doing amiss of one's burden, it is to be expected that such a process of malformation and misinterpretation will, at the very least, produce deviations in style between strong poets. Let us remember always Emerson's insistence as to what it is that makes a poem:

> For it is not meters, but a meter-making argument that makes a poem,—a thought so passionate and alive that like the spirit of a plant or an animal it has an architecture of its own, and adorns nature with a new thing. The thought and the form are equal in the order of time, but in the order of genesis the thought is prior to the form. The poet has a new thought; he has a whole new experience to unfold; he will tell us how it was with him, and all men will be the richer in his fortune. For the experience of each new age requires a new confession, and the world seems always waiting for its poet. . . .

Emerson would not acknowledge that meter-making arguments themselves were subject to the tyrannies of inheritance, but that they are so subject is the saddest truth I know about poets and poetry. In Hardy's best poems, the central meter-making argument is what might be called a skeptical lament for the hopeless incongruity of ends and means in all human acts. Love and the means of love cannot be brought together, and the truest name for the human condition is simply that it is loss:

> And brightest things that are theirs. . . .
> Ah, no; the years, the years;
> Down their carved names the raindrop plows.

These are the closing lines of *During Wind and Rain*, as good a poem as our century has given us. The poem, like so many others, is a grandchild of the *Ode to the West Wind*, as much as Stevens'

The Course of a Particular or any number of major lyrics by Yeats. A carrion-eater, Old Style, would challenge my observations, and to such a challenge I could offer, in its own terms, only the first appearance of the refrain:

> Ah, no; the years O!
> How the sick leaves reel down in throngs!

But such terms can be ignored. Poetic influence, between strong poets, works in the depths, as all love antithetically works. At the center of Hardy's verse, whether in the early *Wessex Poems* or the late *Winter Words*, is this vision:

> And much I grieved to think how power and will
> In opposition rule our mortal day,

> And why God made irreconcilable
> Good and the means of good; and for despair
> I half disdained mine eyes' desire to fill

> With the spent vision of the times that were
> And scarce have ceased to be—

Shelley's *The Triumph of Life* can give us also the heroic motto for the major characters in Hardy's novels: "For in the battle Life and they did wage,/ She remained conqueror." The motto would serve as well for the superb volume *Winter Words in Various Moods and Metres*, published on October 2 in 1928, the year that Hardy died on January 11. Hardy had hoped to publish the book on June 2, 1928, which would have been his eighty-eighth birthday. Though a few poems in the book go back as far as the 1860's, most were written after the appearance of Hardy's volume of lyrics, *Human Shows*, in 1925. A few books of twentieth-century verse in English compare with *Winter Words* in greatness, but very few. Though the collection is diverse, and has no central design, its emergent theme is a counterpoise to the burden of poetic incarnation, and might be called the Return of the Dead, who haunt Hardy as he faces towards death.

In his early poem (1887), *Shelley's Skylark*, Hardy, writing rather in the style of his fellow Shelleyan, Browning, speaks of his ancestor's "ecstatic heights in thought and rhyme." Recent critics who admire Shelley are not particularly fond of *To a Skylark*, and it is rather too ecstatic for most varieties of modern sensibility, but we can surmise why it so moved Hardy:

> We look before and after,
>   And pine for what is not:
> Our sincerest laughter
> With some pain is fraught;
> Our sweetest songs are those that tell of saddest thought.
>
> Yet if we could scorn
>   Hate, and pride, and fear;
> If we were things born
>   Not to shed a tear,
> I know not how thy joy we ever should come near.

The thought here, as elsewhere in Shelley, is not so simple as it may seem. Our divided consciousness, keeping us from being able to unperplex joy from pain, and ruining the presentness of the moment, at least brings us an aesthetic gain. But even if we lacked our range of negative affections, even if grief were not our birthright, the pure joy of the lark's song would still surpass us. We may think of Shelleyan ladies like Marty South, and even more Sue Bridehead, who seems to have emerged from the *Epipsychidion*. Or perhaps we may remember Angel Clare, as a kind of parody of Shelley himself. Hardy's Shelley is very close to the most central of Shelleys, the visionary skeptic, whose head and whose heart could never be reconciled, for they both told truths, but contrary truths. In *Prometheus Unbound*, we are told that in our life the shadow cast by love is always ruin, which is the head's report, but the heart in Shelley goes on saying that if there is to be coherence at all, it must come through Eros.

Winter Words, as befits a man going into his later eighties, is more in ruin's shadow than in love's realm. The last poem, written in 1927, is called *He Resolves To Say No More*, and follows directly on *"We Are Getting to The End,"* which may be the bleakest sonnet in the language. Both poems explicitly reject any vision of hope, and are set against the Shelleyan rational meliorism of *Prometheus Unbound*. "We are getting to the end of visioning/The impossible within this universe," Hardy flatly insists, and he recalls Shelley's vision of rolling time backward, only to dismiss it as the doctrine of Shelley's Ahasuerus: "(Magians who drive the midnight quill/With brain aglow/Can see it so)". Behind this rejection is the mystery of misprision, of deep poetic influence in its final phase, which I have called *Apophrades* or the Return of the Dead. Hovering everywhere in *Winter Words*, though far less explicitly than it hovers in *The Dynasts*, is Shelley's *Hellas*. The peculiar strength and achievement of *Winter Words* is not that we are compelled to remember Shelley when we read in it, but rather that it makes us read much of Shelley as though Hardy were Shelley's ancestor, the dark father whom the revolutionary idealist failed to cast out.

Nearly every poem in *Winter Words* has a poignance unusual even in Hardy, but I am moved most by *He Never Expected Much*, the poet's reflection on his eighty-sixth birthday, where his dialogue with the "World" attains a resolution:

> "I do not promise overmuch,
>   Child; overmuch;
> Just neutral-tinted haps and such,"
>   You said to minds like mine.
> Wise warning for your credit's sake!
> Which I for one failed not to take,
> And hence could stem such strain and ache
>   As each year might assign.

The "neutral-tinted haps," so supremely hard to get into poems, are the staple of Hardy's achievement in verse, and contrast both to Wordsworth's "sober coloring" and Shelley's "deep autumnal tone." All through *Winter Words* the attentive reader will hear a chastened return of High Romantic Idealism, but muted into Hardy's tonality. Where Yeats malformed both himself and his High Romantic fathers, Blake and Shelley, in the violences of *Last Poems and Plays*, Hardy more effectively subdued the questing temperaments of his fathers, Shelley and Browning, in *Winter Words*. The wrestling with the great dead is subtler in Hardy, and kinder both to himself and to the fathers.

Hardy's Shelley was essentially the darker poet of *Adonais* and *The Triumph of Life*, though I find more quotations from *The Revolt of Islam* scattered through the novels than from any other single work by Shelley, and I suppose *Hellas* and *Prometheus Unbound* were even more direct, technical influences upon *The Dynasts*. But Hardy was one of those young men who went about in the 1860's carrying a volume of Shelley in his pocket. Quite simply, he identified Shelley's voice with poetry itself, and though he could allow his ironic sense to touch other writers, he kept Shelley inviolate, almost as a kind of secular Christ. His misprision of Shelley, his subversion of Shelley's influence, was an unconscious defense, quite unlike the overt struggle against Shelley of Browning and Yeats.

American poets, far more than British, have rebelled overtly against ancestral voices, partly because of Whitman's example, and also because of Emerson's polemic against the very idea of influence, his insistence that going alone must mean refusing even the good models, and so entails reading primarily as an inventor. Our greater emphasis upon originality has produced inversely a more malevolent anxiety of influence, and our poets consequently misinterpret their precursors more radically than do the British. Hardy's was a gentler case of influence-anxiety than that of any other modern strong poet, for reasons allied, I think, to the astonishing ease of Hardy's initial entrance into his poethood. But

Stevens was as astonishing an instance of late incarnation; fifteen years had to intervene between his undergraduate verse and his first real poem, *Blanche McCarthy*, not written until 1915, when he was nearly thirty-six:

> Look in the terrible mirror of the sky
> And not in this dead glass, which can reflect
> Only the surfaces—the bending arm,
> The leaning shoulder and the searching eye.
>
> Look in the terrible mirror of the sky.
> Oh, bend against the invisible; and lean
> To symbols of descending night; and search
> The glare of revelations going by!
>
> Look in the terrible mirror of the sky.
> See how the absent moon waits in a glade
> Of your dark self, and how the wings of stars,
> Upward, from unimagined coverts, fly.

Here, at his true origin, Stevens is already an involuntary and desperate Transcendentalist, rejecting "the dead glass" of the object-world or Not-Me, and directing his vision to the sky, "terrible mirror" for reflecting either the Giant of one's imagination or the Dwarf of the self's disintegration. But the High Romantic, Shelleyan emblems of imagination, moon and stars, are obscured by the self's darkness and by an inventive faculty still unable to function. Yet the desire for revelations, for an inwardness that might stand up to the sky, is dominant and would prevail.

The Rock would have been Stevens' last book if he had not been persuaded to publish a *Collected Poems*. Less various than *Winter Words*, it goes beyond Hardy with several works of a final sublimity: *Madame La Fleurie, To an Old Philosopher in Rome, The World as Meditation, The Rock* itself, and most of all, *The River of Rivers in Connecticut*. These last visions are all Returns of the Dead, final re-captures of priority from a complex precursor, a composite figure at once English and American, but consistently Romantic: Wordsworth, Keats, Shelley, Emerson, Whitman. Whitman is most pervasive, as large a hidden form in Stevens as Shelley was in Hardy. The poet of *The Sleepers* and of the elegy for Lincoln is so stationed in *The Rock*'s cadences and gestures that a reading of Whitman now finds him shadowed by Stevens. *Madame La Fleurie*, Stevens' fearful vision of the earth's final form, is Whitman's terrible mother let loose upon the land. The ultimate revisioning of the inventors of an American Sublime—Emerson and Whitman—is most effective in the wholly solipsistic and new vitalism that rises up as the "unnamed flowing"—of "the river that flows nowhere, like a sea," a river of the heightened senses with a "propelling force" that would prevent even Charon from crossing it. In Stevens' strange, triumphantly isolated joy at the end, as in Hardy's sublimely grim and solitary refusal to sorrow in sorrow, there is the accent of a strong poet who has completed the dialectic of misprision, as Yeats could not quite complete it. Stevens and Hardy weathered their wrestling with the dead, and either could have said at the end what Stevens said, when he saw himself alone with his book as a heterocosm, a finished version of the self or *The Planet on the Table*:

> His self and the sun were one
> And his poems, although makings of his self,
> Were no less makings of the sun.

No less were they makings of the precursor, but the Wars of Eden had been fought, and the hard, partial victory had been won.

2

The dialectics of poetic tradition

Emerson chose three mottos for his most influential essay, "Self-Reliance." The first, from the *Satires* of Persius: "Do not seek yourself outside yourself." The second, from Beaumont and Fletcher:

> Man is his own star; and the soul that can
> Render an honest and a perfect man,
> Commands all light, all influence, all fate;
> Nothing to him falls early or too late. . . .

The third, one of Emerson's own gnomic verses, is prophetic of much contemporary shamanism:

> Cast the bantling on the rocks,
> Suckle him with the she-wolf's teat,
> Wintered with the hawk and fox,
> Power and speed be hands and feet.

Like the fierce, rhapsodic essay they precede, these mottos are addressed to young Americans, men and women, of 1840, who badly needed to be told that they were not latecomers. But we, in fact, *are* latecomers (as indeed they were), and we are better off for consciously knowing it, at least right now. Emerson's single aim was to awaken his auditors to a sense of their own potential *power of making*. To serve his tradition now, we need to counsel a *power of conserving*.

"The hint of the dialectic is more valuable than the dialectic itself," Emerson once remarked, but I intend to contradict him on that also, and to sketch some aspects of the dialectics of literary tradition. Modernism in literature has not passed; rather, it has been exposed as never having been there. Gossip grows old and becomes myth; myth grows older, and becomes dogma. Wyndham Lewis, Eliot and Pound gossiped with one another; the New Criticism aged them into a myth of Modernism; now the antiquarian Hugh Kenner has dogmatized this myth into the Pound Era, a canon of accepted titans. Pretenders to godhood Kenner roughly reduces to their mortality; the grand triumph of Kenner is his judgment that Wallace Stevens represented the culmination of the poetics of Edward Lear.

Yet this is already dogma grown antique: Post-Modernism also has its canons and its canonizers; and I find myself surrounded by living classics, in recently dead poets of strong ambition and hysterical intensity, and in hyperactive novelist non-novelists, who are I suppose the proper seers for their armies of student non-students. I discover it does little good these days to remind literary students that Cowley, Cleveland, Denham and Waller were for generations considered great poets, or that much of the best contemporary opinion preferred Campbell, Moore and Rogers to John Keats. And I would fear to tell students that while I judge Ruskin to have been the best critic of the nineteenth century, he did proclaim *Aurora Leigh* by Mrs. Browning to be the best long poem of that century. Great critics nod, and entire generations go wrong in judging their own achievements. Without what Shelley called a being washed in the blood of the Great Redeemer, Time, literary tradition appears powerless to justify its own selectivities. Yet if tradition cannot establish its own centrality, it becomes something other than the liberation from time's chaos it implicitly promised to be. Like all convention, it moves from an idealized function to a stifling or blocking tendency.

I intend here to reverse Emerson (though I revere him) and to assert for literary tradition its currently pragmatic as opposed to idealized function: it is now valuable precisely because it partly blocks, because it stifles the weak, because it represses even the strong. To study literary tradition today is to achieve a dangerous but enabling act of the mind that works against all ease in fresh "creation." Kierkegaard could afford to believe that he became great in proportion to striven-with greatness, but we come later. Nietzsche insisted that nothing was more pernicious than the sense of being a latecomer, but I want to insist upon the contrary: nothing is now more salutary than such a sense. Without it, we cannot distinguish between the energy of humanistic performance and merely organic energy, which never alas needs to be saved from itself.

I remember, as a young man setting out to be a university teacher, how afflicted I was by my sense of uselessness, my not exactly vitalizing fear that my chosen profession reduced to an incoherent blend of antiquarianism and culture-mongering. I recall also that I would solace myself by thinking that while a scholar-teacher of literature could do no good, at least he could do no harm, or anyway not to others, whatever he did to himself. But that was at the very start of the decade of the fifties, and after more than twenty years I have come to understand that I under-rated my profession, as much in its capacity for doing harm as in its potential for good works. Even our treasons, our betrayals of our implicit trusts, are treasons of something more than of the intellectuals, and most directly damage our immediate students, our Oedipal sons and daughters. Our profession is not genuinely akin any longer to that of the historians or the philosophers. Without willing the change, our theoretical critics have become negative theologians, our practical critics are close to being Agaddic commentators, and all of our teachers, of whatever generation, teach how to live, what to do, in order to avoid the damnation of death-in-life. I do not believe that I am talking about an ideology, nor am I acknowledging any shade whatsoever of the recent Marxist critiques of our profession. Whatever the academic profession of letters now is on the Continent (shall we say an anthropology half-Marxist, half-Buddhist?) or in Britain (shall we say a middle-class amateurism displacing an aristocratic amateurism?), it is currently in America a wholly Emersonian phenomenon. Emerson abandoned his church to become a secular orator, rightly trusting that the lecture, rather than the sermon, was the proper and luminous melody for Americans. We have institutionalized Emerson's procedures, while abandoning (understandably) his aims, for the burden of his prophecy is already carried by our auditors.

Northrop Frye, who increasingly looks like the Proclus or Iamblichus of our day, has Platonized the dialectics of tradition, its relation to fresh creation, into what he calls the Myth of Concern, which turns out to be a Low Church version of T. S. Eliot's Anglo-Catholic myth of Tradition and the Individual Talent. In Frye's reduction, the student discovers that he becomes something, and thus uncovers or demystifies himself, by first being persuaded that tradition is inclusive rather than exclusive, and so makes a place for him. The student is a cultural assimilator who *thinks* because he has *joined* a larger body of thought. Freedom, for Frye as for Eliot, is the change, however slight, that any genuine single consciousness brings about in the order of literature simply by joining the simultaneity of such order. I confess that I no longer understand this simultaneity, except as a fiction that Frye, like Eliot, passes upon himself. This fiction is a noble idealization, and as a lie against time will go the way of every noble idealization. Such positive thinking served many purposes during the sixties, when continuities, of any kind, badly required to be summoned, even if they did not come to our call. Wherever we are bound, our dialectical development now seems invested in the interplay of repetition and discontinuity, and needs a very different sense of what our stance is in regard to literary tradition.

All of us now have been pre-empted, as I think we are all quite uneasily aware. We are rueful that we are asked ("compelled" might be more accurate) to pay for the discontents not only of the

civilization we enjoy, but of the civilization of all previous genera-
tions from whom we have inherited. Literary tradition, once we
even contemplate entering its academies, now insists upon being
our "family history," and inducts us into its "family romance" in
the unfortunate role prefigured by Browning's Childe Roland, a
candidate for heroism who aspired only to fail at least as miserably
as his precursors failed. There are no longer any archetypes to dis-
place; we have been ejected from the imperial palace whence we
came, and any attempt to find a substitute for it will not be a be-
nign displacement but only another culpable trespass, neither more
nor less desperate than any Oedipal return to origins. For us, crea-
tive emulation of literary tradition leads to images of inversion, in-
cest, sado-masochistic parody, of which the great, gloriously self-
defeating master is Pynchon, whose *Gravity's Rainbow* is a perfect
text for the sixties, Age of Frye and Borges, but already deliberately
belated for the seventies. Substitute-gratifications and myths-of-
displacement turn out to be an identity in Pynchon's book.

Gershom Scholem has an essay on "Tradition and New Creation
in the Ritual of the Kabbalists" that reads like a prescription for
Pynchon's novel, and I suspect Pynchon found another source in
it. The magical formula of the Kabbalistic view of ritual, according
to Scholem, is as follows: "everything not only *is in* everything else
but also *acts upon* everything else." Remind yourself that Kabbalah
literally means "tradition," that which has been received, and
reflect on the extraordinary over-determination and stupefying
over-organization that a Kabbalistic book like *Gravity's Rainbow* is
condemned to manifest. I will mention Kabbalism and its over-
relevances again later in this chapter, but need first to de-
mythologize and de-esotericize my own view of literary tradition.
The proper starting point for any de-mystification has to be a re-
turn to the commonal. Let me ask then: what is literary tradition?
What is a classic? What is a canonical view of tradition? How are
canons of accepted classics formed, and how are they unformed?
I think that all these quite traditional questions can take one sim-

plistic but still dialectical question as their summing-up: do we choose a tradition or does it choose us, and why is it necessary that a choosing take place, or a being chosen? What happens if one tries to write, or to teach, or to think, or even to read without the sense of a tradition?

Why, nothing at all happens, just nothing. You cannot write or teach or think or even read without imitation, and what you imitate is what another person has done, that person's writing or teaching or thinking or reading. Your relation to what informs that person *is* tradition, for tradition is influence that extends past one generation, a carrying-over of influence. Tradition, the Latin *traditio*, is etymologically a handing-over or a giving-over, a delivery, a giving-up and so even a surrender or a betrayal. *Traditio* in our sense is Latin only in language; the concept deeply derives from the Hebraic *Mishnah*, an oral handing-over, or transmission of oral precedents, of what has been found to work, of what has been instructed successfully. Tradition is good teaching, where "good" means pragmatic, instrumental, fecund. But how primal is teaching, in comparison to writing? Necessarily, the question is rhetorical; whether or not the psychic Primal Scene is the one where we were begotten, and whether or not the societal Primal Scene is the murder of a Sacred Father by rival sons, I would venture that the artistic Primal Scene *is* the trespass of teaching. What Jacques Derrida calls the Scene of Writing itself depends upon a Scene of Teaching, and poetry is crucially pedagogical in its origins and function. Literary tradition begins when a fresh author is simultaneously cognizant not only of his own struggle against the forms and presence of a precursor, but is compelled also to a sense of the Precursor's place in regard to what came before *him*.

Ernst Robert Curtius, in the best study of literary tradition I have ever read, his definitive *European Literature and the Latin Middle Ages* (1948), concluded that "like all life, tradition is a vast passing away and renewal." But even Curtius, who could accept his own wisdom, cautioned us that Western literary tradition could be apprehended clearly "only" for the twenty-five centuries from Homer to Goethe; for the two centuries after Goethe we still could not know what was canonical or not. The later Enlightenment, Romanticism, Modernism, Post-Modernism; all these, by implication, are one phenomenon and we still cannot know precisely whether or not that phenomenon possesses continuity rather than primarily discontinuity in regard to the tradition between Homer and Goethe. Nor are there Muses, nymphs who *know*, still available to tell us the secrets of continuity, for the nymphs certainly are now departing. I prophesy though that the first true break with literary continuity will be brought about in generations to come, if the burgeoning religion of Liberated Woman spreads from its clusters of enthusiasts to dominate the West. Homer will cease to be the inevitable precursor, and the rhetoric and forms of our literature then may break at last from tradition.

It remains not arbitrary nor even accidental to say that everyone who now reads and writes in the West, of whatever racial background, sex or ideological camp, is still a son or daughter of Homer. As a teacher of literature who prefers the morality of the Hebrew Bible to that of Homer, indeed who prefers the Bible aesthetically to Homer, I am no happier about this dark truth than you are, if you happen to agree with William Blake when he passionately cries aloud that it is Homer and Virgil, the Classics, and not the Goths and Vandals that fill Europe with wars. But how did this truth, whether dark or not, impose itself upon us?

All continuities possess the paradox of being absolutely arbitrary in their origins, and absolutely inescapable in their teleologies. We know this so vividly from what we all of us oxymoronically call our love lives that its literary counterparts need little demonstration. Though each generation of critics rightly re-affirms the aesthetic supremacy of Homer, he is so much part of the aesthetic *given* for them (and us) that the re-affirmation is a redundancy. What we call "literature" is inescapably connected to education by a continuity of twenty-five hundred years, a continuity that began in the sixth century B.C. when Homer first became a schoolbook for the Greeks, or as Curtius says simply and definitively: "Homer, for them, was the 'tradition.'" When Homer became a schoolbook, literature became a school subject quite permanently. Again, Curtius makes the central formulation: "Education becomes the medium of the literary tradition: a fact which is characteristic of Europe, but which is not necessarily so in the nature of things."

This formulation is worth considerable dialectical investigation, particularly in a time as educationally confused as ours recently has been. Nothing in the literary world even sounds quite so silly to me as the passionate declarations that poetry must be liberated from the academy, declarations that would be absurd at any time, but peculiarly so some twenty-five hundred years after Homer and the academy first became indistinguishable. For the answer to the question "What is literature?" must begin with the word "literature," based on Quintilian's word *litteratura* which was his translation of the Greek *grammatike*, the art of reading and writing conceived as a dual enterprise. Literature, and the study of literature, were in their origin a single, unified concept. When Hesiod and Pindar invoke the Muses, they do so *as students*, so as to enable themselves *to teach their readers*. When the first literary scholars wholly distinct from poets created their philology in Alexandria, they began by classifying and then selecting authors, canonizing according to secular principles clearly ancestral in relation to our own. The question we go on asking—"What is a classic?"—they first answered for us by reducing the tragedians initially to five, and later to three. Curtius informs us that the name *classicus* first appears very late, under the Antonine emperors, meaning literary citizens of the first class, but the concept of classification was itself Alexandrian. We are Alexandrians still, and we may as well be proud of it, for it is central to our profession. Even "Modernism," a shibboleth many of us think we may have invented, is necessarily an Alexandrian inheritance also. The scholar Aristarchus, working at the Museion in Alexandria, first contrasted the *neoteroi* or "moderns" with

Homer, in defense of a latecomer poet like Callimachus. *Modernus,* based on the word *modo,* for "now," first came into use in the sixth century A.D., and it is worth remembering that "Modernism" always means "For Now."

Alexandria, which thus founded our scholarship, permanently set the literary tradition of the school, and introduced the secularized notion of the canon, though the actual term of canon for "catalogue" of authors was not used until the eighteenth century. Curtius, in his wonderfully comprehensive researches, ascribes the first canon-formation in a modern vernacular, secular literature to the sixteenth-century Italians. The French in the seventeenth century followed, establishing their permanent version of classicism, a version that the English Augustans bravely but vainly tried to emulate before they were flooded out by that great English renaissance of the English Renaissance we now call the Age of Sensibility or the Sublime, and date fairly confidently from the mid-1740's. This renaissance of the Renaissance was and is Romanticism, which is of course *the* tradition of the last two centuries. Canon-formation, for us, has become a part of Romantic tradition, and our still-current educational crisis in the West is rather clearly only another Romantic epicycle, part of the continuity of upheaval that began with revolution in the West Indies and America, spread to France and through her to the Continent, and thence to Russia, Asia and Africa in our time. Just as Romanticism and Revolution became one composite form, so the dialectic of fresh canon-formation joining itself to a gradual ideological reversal endures into this current decade.

But Romantic tradition differs vitally from earlier forms of tradition, and I think this difference can be reduced to a useful formula. Romantic tradition is *consciously late,* and Romantic literary psychology is therefore necessarily a *psychology of belatedness.* The romance-of-trespass, of violating a sacred or daemonic ground, is a central form in modern literature, from Coleridge and Wordsworth to the present. Whitman follows Emerson by insisting that he strikes up for a new world, yet the guilt of belatedness haunts him and all of his American literary descendants. Yeats was early driven into Gnostic evasions of nature by a parallel guilt, and even the apocalyptic Lawrence is most persuasive when he follows his own analyses of Melville and Whitman to trumpet the doom of what he calls our white race with its hideously belated aversion from what he oddly insisted upon calling blood-consciousness. Romanticism, more than any other tradition, is appalled by its own overt continuities, and vainly but perpetually fantasizes some end to repetitions.

This Romantic psychology of belatedness, from which Emerson failed to save us, his American descendants, is the cause, in my judgment, of the excessively volatile senses-of-tradition that have made canon-formation so uncertain a process during the last two centuries, and particularly during the last twenty years. Take some contemporary examples. A quick way to start a quarrel with any current group of critics would be to express my conviction that Robert Lowell is anything but a permanent poet, that he has been mostly a maker of period-pieces from his origins until now. Similarly, as violent a quarrel would ensue if I expressed my judgment that Norman Mailer is so flawed a writer that his current enshrinement among academics is the largest single index to our current sense of belatedness. Lowell and Mailer, however I rate them, are at least conspicuous literary energies. It would lead to something more intense than quarrels if I expressed my judgment upon "black poetry" or the "literature of Women's Liberation." But quarrels, or even abuse, is all such *obiter dicta* could lead to, for our mutual sense of canonical standards has undergone a remarkable dimming, a fading into the light of a common garishness. Revisionism, always a Romantic energizer, has become so much a norm that even rhetorical standards seem to have lost their efficacy. Literary tradition has become the captive of the revisionary impulse, and I think we must go past viewing-with-alarm if we are to understand this quite inescapable phenomenon, the subsuming of tradition by belatedness.

The revisionary impulse, in writing and in reading, has a directly inverse relationship to our psychological confidence in what I am calling the Scene of Instruction. Milton's Satan, who remains the greatest really Modern or Post-Enlightenment poet in the language, can give us a paradigm of this inverse relationship. The ultimate Scene of Instruction is described by Raphael in Book V of *Paradise Lost*, where God proclaims to the Angels that "This day I have begot whom I declare/My only son" and provocatively warns that "him who disobeys/Mee disobeys . . . /and . . . falls/Into utter darkness." We can describe this as an imposition of the psychology of belatedness, and Satan, like any strong poet, declines to be merely a latecomer. His way of returning to origins, of making the Oedipal trespass, is to become a rival creator to God-as-creator. He embraces Sin as his Muse, and begets upon her the highly original poem of Death, the only poem that God will permit him to write.

Let me reduce my own allegory, or my allegorical interpretation of Satan, by invoking a wonderful poem of Emily Dickinson's, "The Bible is an antique Volume—" (no. 1545), in which she calls Eden "the ancient Homestead," Satan "the Brigadier," and Sin "a distinguished Precipice/Others must resist." As a heretic whose orthodoxy was Emersonianism, Dickinson recognized in Satan a distinguished precursor gallantly battling against the psychology of belatedness. But then, Dickinson and Emerson wrote in an America that needed, for a while, to battle against the European exhaustions of history. I am temperamentally a natural revisionist, and I respond to Satan's speeches more strongly than to any other poetry I know, so it causes some anguish in me to counsel that currently we need Milton's sense of tradition much more than Emerson's revisionary tradition. Indeed, the counsel of necessity must be taken further: most simply, we need Milton, and not the Romantic return of the repressed Milton but the Milton who made his great poem identical with the process of repression that is vital to literary tradition. But a resistance even in myself is set up by my counsel of necessity, because even I want to know: what do I mean by "we"? Teachers? Students? Writers? Readers?

I do not believe that these are separate categories, nor do I believe that sex, race, social class can narrow this "we" down. If we are human, then we depend upon a Scene of Instruction, which is necessarily also a scene of authority and of priority. If you will not have one instructor or another, then precisely by rejecting all instructors, you will condemn yourself to the earliest Scene of Instruction that imposed itself upon you. The clearest analogue is necessarily Oedipal; reject your parents vehemently enough, and you will become a belated version of them, but compound with their reality, and you may partly free yourself. Milton's Satan failed, particularly as poet, after making a most distinguished beginning, because he became only a parody of the bleakest aspects of Milton's God. I greatly prefer Pynchon to Mailer as a writer because a voluntary parody is more impressive than an involuntary one, but I wonder if our aesthetic possibilities need to be reduced now to just such a choice. Do the dialectics of literary tradition condemn us, at this time, either to an affirmation of belatedness, via Kabbalistic inversion, or to a mock-vitalistic lie-against-time, via an emphasis upon the self-as-performer?

I cannot answer this hard question, because I am uneasy with the current alternatives to the ways of Pynchon and of Mailer, at least in fictional or quasi-fictional prose. Saul Bellow, with all his literary virtues, clearly shows the primal exhaustions of being a latecomer rather more strenuously in his way than Pynchon or Mailer do in theirs. I honestly don't enjoy Bellow more, and I would hesitate to find anything universal in such enjoyment even if I had it. Contemporary American poetry seems healthier to me, and provides alternatives to the voluntary parodies that Lowell has given us, or the involuntary parodies at which Ginsberg is so prominent. Yet even the poets I most admire, John Ashbery and A. R. Ammons, are rendered somewhat problematic by a cultural situation of such belatedness that literary survival itself seems fairly questionable. As Pynchon says in the closing pages of his uncanny book: "You've got much older. . . . Fathers are carriers of the virus of Death, and sons are the infected. . . ." And he adds a little further on in his Gospel of Sado-anarchism that this time we *"will* arrive, my God, too late."

I am aware that this must seem a Gospel of Gloom, and no one ought to be asked to welcome a kakangelist, a bearer of ill-tidings. But I cannot see that evasions of Necessity benefit anyone, least of all educationally. The teacher of literature now in America, far more than the teacher of history or philosophy or religion, is condemned to teach the presentness of the past, because history, philosophy and religion have withdrawn as agents from the Scene of Instruction, leaving the bewildered teacher of literature alone at the altar, terrifiedly wondering whether he is to be sacrifice or priest. If he evades his burden by attempting to teach only the supposed presence of the present, he will find himself teaching only some simplistic, partial reduction that wholly obliterates the present in the name of one or another historicizing formula, or past injustice, or dead faith, whether secular or not. Yet how is he to teach a tradition now grown so wealthy and so heavy that to accommodate it demands more strength than any single consciousness can provide, short of the parodistic Kabbalism of a Pynchon?

All literary tradition has been necessarily élitist, in every period, if only because the Scene of Instruction always depends upon a primal choosing and a being chosen, which is what "élite" means. Teaching, as Plato knew, is necessarily a branch of erotics, in the wide sense of desiring what we have not got, of redressing our poverty, of compounding with our fantasies. No teacher, however impartial he or she attempts to be, can avoid choosing among students, or being chosen by them, for this is the very nature of teaching. Literary teaching is precisely like literature itself; no strong writer can choose his precursors until first he is chosen by them, and no strong student can fail to be chosen by his teachers. Strong students, like strong writers, will find the sustenance they must have. And strong students, like strong writers, will rise in the most unexpected places and times, to wrestle with the internalized violence pressed upon them by their teachers and precursors.

Yet our immediate concern, as I am aware, is hardly with the strong, but with the myriads of the many, as Emersonian democracy seeks to make its promises a little less deceptive than they have been. Do the dialectics of literary tradition yield us no wisdom that can help with the final burden of the latecomer, which is the extension of the literary franchise? What is the particular inescapability of literary tradition for the teacher who must go out to find himself as a voice in the wilderness? Is he to teach *Paradise Lost* in preference to the Imamu Amiri Baraka?

I think these questions are self-answering, or rather will be, with the passage of only a few more years. For the literary teacher, more than ever, will find he is teaching *Paradise Lost*, and the other central classics of Western literary tradition, whether he is teaching them overtly or not. The psychology of belatedness is unsparing, and the Scene of Instruction becomes ever more primal as our society sags around us. Instruction, in our late phase, becomes an antithetical process almost in spite of itself, and for antithetical teaching you require antithetical texts, that is to say, texts antithetical to your students as well as to yourself and to other texts. Milton's Satan may stand as representative of the entire canon when he challenges us to challenge Heaven with him, and he will provide the truest handbook for all those, of whatever origin, who as he says "with ambitious mind/Will covet more." Any teacher of the dispossessed, of those who assert *they* are the insulted and injured, will serve the deepest purposes of literary tradition and meet also the deepest needs of his students when he gives them possession of Satan's grand opening of the Debate in Hell, which I cite now to close this chapter on the dialectics of tradition:

> With this advantage then
> To union, and firm Faith, and firm accord,
> More than can be in Heav'n, we now return
> To claim our just inheritance of old,
> Surer to prosper than prosperity
> Could have assur'd us; and by what best way,
> Whether of open War or covert guile,
> We now debate; who can advise, may speak.

3

The primal scene of instruction

The LORD spoke with you face to face in the mount out of the midst of the fire—I stood between the LORD and you at that time, to declare unto you the word of the LORD; for ye were afraid because of the fire, and went not up into the mount—

Deuteronomy 5:4-5

. . . A tradition based only on oral communication could not produce the obsessive character which appertains to religious phenomena. It would be listened to, weighed, and perhaps rejected, just like any other news from outside; it would never achieve the privilege of being freed from the coercion of logical thinking. It must first have suffered the fate of repression, the state of being unconscious, before it could produce such mighty effects on its return. . . .

Freud, Moses and Monotheism
(Vintage ed., 129)

Back from Babylon, Ezra, as scribe of the Return, resolved that his people were to seek always the presence of the Book. The primacy of the Book, and of the Oral Tradition as its interpretation, dates from this heroic resolution of the mid fifth century B.C. Ezra rightly saw himself as a continuator and not as a point of origin, a strong scribe rather than a strong poet:

> This Ezra went up from Babylon; and he was a ready scribe in the law of Moses, which the LORD God of Israel had given: and the king granted him all his request, according to the hand of the LORD his God upon him. . . .
> For Ezra had prepared his heart to seek the law of the LORD, and to do it, and to teach in Israel statutes and judgments.
>
> *Ezra* 7:6, 10

"To seek" here translates *lidrosh*, for which a fuller rendering is "to interpret." Interpretation, *Midrash*, is a seeking for the Torah, but more in the mode of making the Torah larger than in opening it to the bitterness of experience. The *Soferim* or Men of the Book, the true Scribes, centered authority upon the Book, insisting that everything was already in it, necessarily including all of their readings. Torah was true text, and their interpretations did not falsify it, but gave it context, and always through contemporary authority, "the judge that shall be in those days."

Midrash originally was Oral Tradition, and persisted with this bias against writing-down for centuries. Oral Tradition depends upon memory, personality, and the direct tradition of teachers who in turn taught teachers. Perhaps the *Soferim* at first were inhibited by the fear that interpretation might substitute for text, yet this is unlikely. Certainly, the dialectical nature of Oral Tradition fears loss when writing-down begins to dominate, for writing limits dialectic, which is as much a *Midrashic* as a Socratic realization. The great Rabbis feared reduction as much as Socrates did, but more as a purely pedagogic than as a philosophical menace.

Yet the Jewish Oral Tradition, with its only apparent valorization of speech over writing, seems to me wholly at variance with Platonic tradition in the same area. Thorleif Boman, in his study *Hebrew Thought Compared with Greek*, contrasts the Hebrew word for "word," *davhar*, with the Greek word for "word," *logos*. *Davhar* is at once "word," "thing" and "act," and its root meaning involves the notion of driving forward something that initially is held-back. This is the word as a moral act, a true word that is at once an object or thing and a deed or act. A word not an act or thing is thus a lie, something that was behind and was not driven forward. In contrast to this dynamic word, the *logos* is an intellectual concept, going back to a root meaning that involves gathering, arranging, putting-into-order. The concept of *davhar* is: speak, act, be. The concept of *logos* is: speak, reckon, think. *Logos* orders and makes reasonable the context of speech, yet in its deepest meaning does not deal with the function of speaking. *Davhar*, in thrusting forward what is concealed in the self, is concerned with oral expression, with getting a word, a thing, a deed out into the light.

Socrates, praising dialectic in the *Phaedrus*, exalted "words founded on knowledge, words which can defend both themselves and him who planted them, words which instead of remaining barren contain a seed whence new words grow up in new characters, whereby the seed is vouchsafed immortality." Philosophy and literature alike nobly assert this Socratic exaltation as ancestor, at least until Nietzsche. From Nietzsche descends the tradition that culminates in Jacques Derrida, whose deconstructive enterprise questions this "logocentric enclosure" and seeks to demonstrate that the spoken word is less primal than writing is. Writing, in Derrida's vision, is what makes memory possible, in the sense that memory enables the continuance of thought, allows thought a subject matter. Writing, as Derrida tropes it, both keeps us from the void and, more aggressively (as against voicing), gives us a saving difference, by preventing that coincidence of speaker with subject that would entrap us in a presence so total as to stop the mind. Derrida's coinage, *différance*, combines "to differ" and "to defer" into a verb of interplay, one that relates signs only to other signs, earlier and later, signs that are seen as having been generated aboriginally, primally, by the articulation of marks that is language. Though he nowhere says so, it may be that Derrida is substituting *davhar* for *logos*, thus correcting Plato by a Hebraic equating of the writing-act and the mark-of-articulation with the word itself. Much of Derrida is in the spirit of the great Kabbalist interpreters of Torah, interpreters who create baroque mythologies out of those elements in Scripture that appear least homogeneous in the sacred text.

The Kabbalistic emphasis on an esoteric Oral Tradition was absolute, climaxing in the paradox that we know the doctrines of Isaac Luria, most inventive of all Kabbalists, only through the competing versions of various disciples, some of whom never knew

Luria. This makes Lurianic or later Kabbalah as well as its Hasidic descendant a bewildering labyrinth that cannot be understood conceptually, strictly on the basis of reading and interpreting texts. The *Zohar*, most influential of Kabbalistic texts (and particularly so for Luria) taught that the Tables of the Law as handed down from Moses were a second Torah, the first and "uncreated Torah" being concealed from us except as the esoteric or Kabbalistic version of Oral Tradition. This tradition or "reception" (which is what the word *Kabbalah* means) is spoken of as "a hammer shattering stone," the stone being Written Torah. The *Zohar* cites Exodus 20:18: "And all the people saw the thunderings, and the lightnings, and the noise of the trumpet, and the mountain smoking: and when the people saw it, they removed, and stood afar off." In the *Zohar*'s interpretation, this means that the Israelites confronted divine words inscribed on the darkness of the holy cloud that masked God's actual presence, and so God's script simultaneously was heard as Oral Tradition and seen as Written Torah.

I have cited Kabbalah as analogue to Derrida, but Oral Tradition was no more to be subsumed by Kabbalah than the Written Tradition was to yield itself to esoteric authors. Oral Tradition descended in a direct line from Ezra to the Pharisees and on to the main Rabbinical continuity. The central text for Oral Tradition, if this only apparent paradox be granted, is the *Pirke Aboth*, Sayings or Wisdom of the Fathers, particularly in its magnificent opening:

> Moses received Torah from Sinai and delivered it to Joshua, and Joshua to the Elders, and the Elders to the Prophets, and the Prophets delivered it to the Men of the Great Synagogue. These said three things; Be deliberate in judging, and raise up many disciples, and make a hedge about the Torah.

Travers Herford, in his commentary on *Aboth*, emphasizes the delivering of these opening maxims by the Men of the Great Synagogue, rather than injunctions given by earlier and more undisputed figures in the tradition. The *Aboth* proper, the Fathers of the tradition, begin with the hypothetical Great Synagogue or Academy of Ezra and go down to Hillel in the Pharisaic line. Leo Baeck observed that the Talmudic phrase "a hedge about the Torah" refers to the defense of a teaching tradition and not to the strict maintenance of custom, law or ritual. In his book *The Pharisees* Herford defended the teaching tradition against the composers of Apocalypses and Apocrypha who were the ancestors of Kabbalah. Against the assertion of R. H. Charles in his *Eschatology* that Apocalyptic writing was "the true child of prophecy," Herford eloquently made a vital and lasting distinction between the teaching tradition of the Talmudists and the revisionist traditions of Apocrypha:

> It is no doubt true that the "Law" did acquire a supreme place in the Judaism of the centuries since Ezra. But, if there had been, during those centuries, any real prophets who felt that they had a word of the Lord to declare, they would have declared it. Who would have prevented them? Certainly not the "Law," nor those who expounded it. Rather, who *could* have prevented them? Amos said what he had to say in spite of the priest and the king; and, if there had been an Amos in the centuries now in question, he would have spoken his word regardless of Pharisee or Scribe, in the very unlikely case of their wishing to prevent him. . . . the Apocalyptic writings are a witness . . . to the feebleness of those who aspired to wear the mantle of Elijah. If their writings had appeared under their own names, it is quite conceivable that no attention would have been paid to them; their device of introducing their works under the shelter of great names—Enoch, Moses, Solomon, Ezra—was one which men of original genius would not have needed nor condescended to use. . . . Their works bear out this opinion, for their want of original power is conspicuous. They are obviously based on the prophetic writings; and, what is more, the peculiar type of Apocalyptic writing is repeated in its main features over and over again. . . .

The difference between a Talmudic work like *Aboth* and an Apocryphal work like the Book of Enoch is the Hebraic version of the Greek difference between *ethos* and *pathos*, a distinction definitive for separating out all orthodox from revisionist traditions. Herford stresses the Talmudic emphasis upon *Halachah*, the "way-to-go" or rule of right conduct as defined by orthodox authority. Apocrypha and Apocalypse leap over *Halachah* in their despair of the present. Contrast at random nearly any maxim of *Aboth* with a characteristic moment of the Book of Enoch. Here is Rabbi Tarphon, condensing much of the *ethos* of the Fathers into a majestic formulation: "He used to say:—'You are not required to complete the work, but neither are you free to desist from it.' " Here is the author of Enoch, in his strained *pathos:* "Grieve not if your soul into Sheol has descended in grief, and that in your life your body fared not according to your goodness, but wait ye for the day of the judgment of sinners, and for the day of cursing and chastisement."

Any competent literary critic who has worked his way through *Aboth* and Enoch will begin to suspect that a strong aesthetic motive was involved in the canonical principle. *Aboth* is neither mere repetition nor revisionism, but is wisdom reliant upon *davhar* and its oral authority. Oral Tradition excludes Apocrypha and Apocalypse in the same way that Torah (except for the Book of Daniel) excluded them: they manifest too palpable an anxiety of influence and consequently too abrupt a revisionary swerve away from the continuities of tradition. And yet, they show us an aspect of individual creativity that canon-formation never reveals, an aspect that can teach us something fundamental yet hidden about the nature of textual meaning, particularly in regard to textual origins.

The prestige of origins is a universal phenomenon, against which a solitary de-mystifier like Nietzsche struggled in vain, though the struggle gave us his most convincing book, *Towards a Genealogy of Morals*, and the most powerful of the aphoristic formulations of *Beyond Good and Evil*. Origin and purpose, Nietzsche insisted, were separate entities that should not be mixed. All sacred history, as Nietzsche knew, was against him, and sacred history has a way of prevailing even in ages and societies where the sacred appears largely through displacement. Mircea Eliade in many of his writings demonstrates the universal prestige of beginnings, to which perfection is always ascribed. A nostalgia for origins governs every primal tradition, and accounts for our continued awe of shamans, who in their ecstasies are assumed to become "those who had memory of the beginnings." Hence, by Eliade's argument, we all of us retain the notion "that it is the first manifestation of a thing that is significant and valid, not its successive epiphanies." The original Time is both strong and sacred, whereas its recurrences progressively become weaker and less holy. Eliade, summing up universal religious history, can be read almost as a direct attack upon Nietzsche when the myth of origins reasserts itself:

> A new state of things always implies a preceding state, and the latter, in the last analysis, is the World. It is from this initial "totality" that the later modifications develop. The cosmic milieu in which one lives, limited as it may be, constitutes the "World"; its "origin" and "history" precede any other individual history. The mythical idea of the "origin" is part and parcel of the mystery of "creation." A thing has an "origin" because it was created, that is, because a power clearly manifested itself in the World, an event took place. In short, the *origin* of a thing accounts for its *creation*.

But how do we pass from origins to repetition and continuity, and thence to the discontinuity that marks all revisionism? Is there not a missing trope we need to restore, another Primal Scene that we are reluctant to confront? I intend here to sketch such a scene, by the means of restoring the trope, which is technically the one that traditional rhetoric has called *metalepsis* or *transumption*.

What makes a scene Primal? A scene is a setting as seen by a viewer, a place where action, whether real or fictitious, occurs or is staged. Every Primal Scene is necessarily a stage performance or fantastic fiction, and when described is necessarily a trope. Freud's two Primal Scenes, of the Oedipal fantasy and of the slaying of a father by his rival sons, are both synecdoches. Philip Rieff names as Freud's master trope his understanding of health through sickness, a remarkably effective synecdoche but one that courts the genetic fallacy. When Freud calls a scene Primal, he rhetorically depends, as Rieff says, upon synecdoche or part-for-whole-substitution as a causal, prior and prefigurative prototype for later psychic development. Since the Primal Scenes are fantasy traumas, they testify to the power of imagination over fact, and indeed give an astonishing preference to imagination over observation. Rieff, following Freud, is compelled to speak of "the true fictions of the interior life." Perhaps this is the oddest paradox of the Freudian vision, since a truly superior psychological reality, the Primal Scene, is warranted only by the imagination. Yet the imagination, as Freud may not have cared to understand, has no referential aspect. It has no meaning in itself because it is not a sign; that is, there is no other sign to which it can relate or be related. Like the *En Sof* or Infinite Godhood of Kabbalah, the imagination stands above and beyond the texts that would invoke it.

Derrida, in his dazzling essay on "Freud and the Scene of Writing," posits a third scene, more Primal than the Freudian synecdoches. Derrida's trope here is the more Sublime one of hyperbole, which has the same close relationship to the defense of repression that synecdoche has to the defenses of reversal and turning-against-the-self. Derrida's argument is that Freud resorts, at decisive moments, to rhetorical models borrowed not from oral tradition, "but from a script which is never subject, extrinsic, and posterior to the spoken word." This script is a visible *agon*, a performance of writing that is at play in all verbal representation. In Derrida's Sublime trope, we are told that "there is no psyche without text," an assertion that goes beyond Derrida's precursor, Lacan, in his grand trope that the structure of the unconscious is linguistic. Psychical life thus is no longer to be represented as a transparency of meaning nor as an opacity of force but as an intra-textual difference in the conflict of meanings and the exertion of forces.

For Derrida, writing is pathbreaking, Freud's *bahnung*, and the psyche is a highway map. Writing breaks its path against resistances, and so the history of the road is seen as identical with the history of writing. Derrida's keenest insight, in my judgment, is that "writing is unthinkable without repression," which is to identify writing-as-such with the daemonizing trope of hyperbole. As Derrida eloquently insists, "we are written only by writing," an hyperbole that destroys the false distinction between reading and writing, and that makes of all literature "the war and ruses between the author who reads and the first reader who dictates." Derrida has made of writing an intra-psychical trope, which is a making that necessarily pleases any reader who himself has made of influence an intra-psychical trope or rather a trope for intra-poetic relationships. Such a reader can find supremely useful Derrida's conclusion that "writing is the scene or stage of history and the play of the world."

Yet Derrida's Scene of Writing is insufficiently Primal both in itself and as exegesis of Freud. It relies, as Freud does, upon a more daring trope, a scheme of transumption or metaleptic reversal that I would name the Primal Scene of Instruction. The way into this Scene can be through the single evasion of Freud's text that seems crucial to Derrida's exegesis. Derrida concludes his essay by quoting a sentence from Freud's *The Problem of Anxiety*:

> If writing—which consists in allowing a fluid to flow out from a tube upon a piece of white paper—has acquired the symbolic meaning of coitus, or if walking has become a symbolic substitute for stamping upon the body of Mother Earth, then both writing and walking will be abstained from, because it is as though forbidden sexual behavior were thereby being indulged in.

Derrida omits the next sentence:

> The ego renounces these functions proper to it in order not to have to undertake a fresh effort of repression, *in order to avoid a conflict with the id*. [Freud's italics.]

With the sentence Derrida does quote, this forms a paragraph. The paragraph following deals with inhibitions that rise in order not to become involved in conflict *with the superego* (Freud's italics again). For Derrida's interpretation of Freud to be correct— that is, for writing to be as primal as coitus—the inhibition of writing would have to come about to avoid a conflict *with the superego, and not with the id.* But *speech, not writing*, as Freud always says, is inhibited to avoid conflict with the superego. For the superego presides over the Scene of Instruction, which is always at least quasi-religious in its associations, and speech therefore is more primal. Writing, which is cognitively secondary, is closer to mere process, to the *automatic* behavior of the id. Freud himself is thus more in the oral than in the writing tradition, unlike Nietzsche and Derrida, who are more purely revisionists, while Freud, perhaps despite himself, is a curiously direct continuator of his people's longest tradition. Freud, unlike Nietzsche and Derrida, knows that precursors become absorbed *into the id* and *not into the superego.* Influence-anxieties of all kinds, with all their afflictions of secondariness, therefore inhibit *writing*, but not nearly so much the oral, logocentric tradition of prophetic speech.

Insofar as Spenser (to move to a literary example) truly was Milton's Great Original, then even Milton was inhibited, for Spenserian vision became an attribute of Milton's id-component. But Milton's prophetic, oral original was Moses, who became an attribute of the Miltonic superego, and thus stimulated the largest power of *Paradise Lost*, which is its marvelous freedom in expanding Scripture to its own purposes. Alastair Fowler usefully notes Milton's emphatic repetition of the word "first," which is employed five times in the opening thirty-three lines of *Paradise Lost.* Moses, as traditionally the *first* Jewish writer, is thus both Milton's authority and his original. Moses "first taught the chosen seed,/In the beginning." The Spirit of God "from the first/Wast present" and Milton asks the Spirit twice to "say first what cause/Moved our grand parents . . . to fall." Satan too is not denied the dignity of his bad priority: "Who first seduced them to that foul revolt?"

The first element to note then about the Scene of Instruction is its absolute firstness; it *defines* priority. Wheeler Robinson, in his study of Old Testament inspiration, moves towards the trope of a Scene of Instruction when he sees that while oral tradition rose to interpret written Torah, written Torah itself as authority replaced cultic acts. The ultimate cultic act is one in which the worshipper receives God's condescension, his accommodating gift of his Election-love. Election-love, God's love for Israel, is the Primal start of a Primal Scene of Instruction, a Scene early displaced from Jewish or Christian into secular and poetic contexts.

Election-love, the Hebrew *'ahabah,* is traced by Norman Snaith to a root that in one form means "to burn or kindle" and in another refers to all kinds of love except familial, whether between husband and wife or child and parent. *'Ahabah* is thus love unconditioned in its giving, but wholly conditioned to passivity in its receiving. Behind any Scene of Writing, at the start of every intertextual encounter, there is this unequal initial love, where necessarily the giving famishes the receiver. The receiver is set on fire, and yet the fire belongs only to the giver.

We must confront here the Romantic version of the dialectic of accommodation, the ironies of which are best expounded by Johann Georg Hamann as precursor, and by his disciple Kierkegaard as heroic ephebe. The grounding of Divine truths in earthly evidences was the ancient mode of accommodation, whether Christian or Neoplatonic. It depended upon a later phase in which the human mind, grateful for such Divine condescension, would observe the proper gradations of ascent back into the heavenly mysteries. Geoffrey Hartman, writing on Milton, distinguishes these as the "authoritarian and initiatory aspects of accommodation," and rightly says that the Romantics wholly rejected the second aspect. Hamann, from 1758 on, pioneered in this rejection, though against his own intent. For Hamann, God's peculiar act of accommodation is in His having condescended to become an author, by dictating to Moses. But reading God's book, whether in Scripture or in nature, does not lead to the traditional ascent by stages but rather to a highly idiosyncratic reading of ciphers, again both in the Bible and in the visible universe. Though accommodation in its root would have us conform with right measure, Hamann is already moving towards an assimilation in which the human receiver incorporates and makes himself one with the Divinely given cipher.

Let us, before passing from Hamann to his descendant, Kierkegaard, examine the dialectic of accommodation and assimilation in modern moralists of the psyche. Sometimes I can believe that Freud (to his dismay) received his largest response from the United States, because Americans recognized in him a formulator of a normative psychology by which they always had been afflicted anyway. I think we can term this a psychology of belatedness, and we can search for its evidences most usefully in our poets, from our origins as a nation until this moment. American poets, rather more than other Western poets, at least since the Enlightenment, are astonishing in their ambitions. Each wants to be the universe, to be the whole of which all other poets are only parts. American psychopoetics are dominated by an American difference from European patterns of the imagination's struggle with its own origins. Our poets' characteristic anxiety is not so much an expectation of being flooded by poetic ancestors, as already *having been* flooded before one could even begin. Emerson's insistence upon Self-Reliance made Whitman and Dickinson and Thoreau possible, and doubtless benefited Hawthorne and Melville despite themselves. But the Scene of Instruction that Emerson sought to void glows with a more and more vivid intensity for contemporary American poets, who enter upon a legacy that paradoxically has accumulated wealth while continuing to insist that it has remained poverty-stricken.

Piaget, in studying the child's cognitive development, has posited a dynamic in which the egocentric infant develops by a progressive decentering until (usually in adolescence) the decentering is complete. The child's space then yields to universal space, and the child's time to history. Having assimilated much of the Not-Me, the child at last accommodates his vision to the vision of others. Poets, we can assume, as children *assimilated* more than the rest of us, and yet somehow *accommodated* less, and so won through the crisis of adolescence without totally decentering. Faced by the Primal Scene of Instruction, even in its poetic variant (where the Idea of Poetry first came to them), they managed to achieve a curious detachment towards crisis that made them capable of a greater attachment to their own wavering centers. In American poets, I surmise, the detachment must be more extreme, and the consequent resistance to decentering greater, for American poets are the most consciously belated in the history of Western poetry.

Freud found it difficult to distinguish evidences of maturation from marks of learning. For Piaget, this problem cannot exist, for he finds it possible, in the areas of imitation and play, to trace a movement from sensory-motor assimilation and accommodation to the origins of representation in a mental assimilation and accommodation. But since our interest is in poetic development, we inherit Freud's difficulty. The interplay between accommodation and assimilation, for us, depends upon the inter-textual covenants that are made, implicitly and explicitly, by later with earlier poets. Necessarily this starts as a covenant of love, though ambivalences enter soon enough. Even as our model for the first phase of a Scene of Instruction came from a distinctive idea of the Old Testament, Election-love or *'ahabah*, so our model for the second phase is drawn from the same source. The model is Covenant-love or *chesed*, the Hebrew word that Miles Coverdale rendered as "lovingkindness" and Luther as *gnade*, which would make it *charis* or "grace." But *chesed*, as Norman Snaith again shows, is difficult to translate. The root means "eagerness" or "sharpness" and the word itself approaches what Freud meant by "antithetical primal words." For the root meaning also embraces that kind of "keenness" that moves from "ardent zeal" to "jealousy," "envy," and "ambition," and so Covenant-love is uneasily allied to a competitive element.

We can deduce, for the purposes of hypothesizing a poetic Primal Scene of Instruction, that the antithetical element in *chesed* leads to the ephebe's first accommodation with the precursor as compared with the absolute assimilation of Election-love. This first accommodation might be called the initial *persona* that the young poet adopts, in the archaic, ritual sense in which the *persona* was the mask representing the *daimonic* or tribal father. Think of Milton as the awesome, blind ancestral bard that he became for the poets of Sensibility and the High Romantics; think of the modern Sublime that he fostered, from Collins to Keats, and a new sense of *daimonic personae* can be surmised.

The third phase in our Primal paradigm must be the rise of an individual inspiration or Muse-principle, a further accommodation of poetic origins to fresh poetic aims. Here the Old Testament *ruach* for "spirit" or "power of God's breath" can be a precise shorthand. To invoke the Muses as spirits or daughters of Zeus was to invoke memory, and so to record and preserve the powers of life already belonging to mankind. But for Christian and post-Christian poets, to invoke *ruach* is to call on a power and life transcending powers already in our control. To differentiate such power from a precursor-source is to pass beyond assimilation once and for all, but also to reject the initiatory or inaugural aspect of the traditional principle of accommodation.

With the fourth phase, the bringing forward of an individual *davhar*, a word one's own that is also one's act and one's veritable presence, poetic incarnation proper has taken place. There remains, in the fifth phase of our scene, the deep sense in which the new poem or poetry is a total interpretation or *lidrosh* of the poem or poetry of origin. In this phase, all of Blake or of Wordsworth becomes a reading or interpretation of all of Milton.

The sixth and final phase of our Primal Scene is revisionism proper, where origins are re-created, or at least a re-creation is attempted, and it is in this phase that a newer practical criticism can begin, at several levels, including the rhetorical. In Chapter 5, I sketch a model of revisionary interpretation as a map of misprision, a charting through revisionary ratios, psychic defenses, rhetorical tropes, and imagistic groupings, of the structure of the typical, central Post-Enlightenment poem. Whereas the first five phases of my Scene of Instruction were canonical in their names and functions, this sixth phase, which is a wholly Romantic accommodation, needs an esoteric paradigm, for which I will turn to the regressive Kabbalah of Isaac Luria, sixteenth-century Rabbi and Saint of Safed.

Luria's dialectics of creation, and their suggestiveness for literary interpretation, were outlined in the Introduction. Here I wish to return again to poetic origins, and to the factors that make a scene Primal. Every Primal Scene is necessarily a fantasy structure, but Freud stumbled badly in positing a phylogenetically transmitted inheritance as the explanation for the universality of such fantasies. His own anxiety, as provoked by Jungian theosophy, compelled him to insist that Primal Scenes were the irreducibly *given*, that they preceded any interpretation to which they gave rise. Against Freud, the idea of the most Primal scene as being a scene of Instruction goes back to the roots of the canonical principle and insists that: "In the beginning was Interpretation," an insistence more Vichian than Nietzschean. Our emphasis is on Vico's "We only know what we ourselves have made" rather than Nietzsche's "Who is the interpreter, and what power does he will to gain over the text?" For even the initial poetic kindling of Election-love is a self-knowing founded on a self-making, since a young Blake or a young Wordsworth had to know a possibility of sublimity in the self before he could know it in Milton and go on to be elected by Milton. The psychic place of heightened consciousness, of intensified demand, where the Scene of Instruction is staged, is necessarily a place cleared by the newcomer in himself, cleared by an initial contraction or withdrawal that makes possible all further self-limitations, and all restituting modes of self-representation. Both the initial and violent excess of demand that is Election-love, and the answering violence of an inadequate response in Covenant-love, are imposed by the new poet upon himself, and both are therefore his interpretations, without which there would be no *given* whatsoever.

For behind all Primal fantasy is the even more Primal repression that Freud both hypothesized and evaded. In *The Case of Schreber* (1911) Freud had described repression as commencing with an act of fixation, meaning merely some inhibition in development. But in the essay on "Repression" (1915) fixation is given a profounder meaning:

> We have reason to assume that there is a *primal repression*, a first phase of repression, which consists in the psychical (ideational) representative of the instinct being denied entrance into the conscious. With this a *fixation* is established; the representative in question persists unaltered from then onwards and the instinct remains attached to it.

Freud was quite unable to explain this fixation, and resorted to the desperate notion that its origin was in some unspecified but very strong archaic experiences that involved "an excessive degree of excitation and the breaking through of the protective shield against stimuli." We need to remember that fixation, for Freud, involves the strong attachment of the libido either to a person or to an imago. To say, as Freud does, that fixation is the basis of repression is to say, in the language of poetic origins, that the trope of hyperbole as a representation of the Sublime begins with the ambivalent love that a newcomer poet feels for his precursor. At the earliest stage he can posit for his own notion of the Primal, Freud too thus relies upon a Scene of Instruction. The unconscious is therefore not a metaphor, but an hyperbole, whose origins are in a more complex trope, indeed in the trope of a trope, the metaleptic or transumptive trope of a Scene of Instruction.

I turn to Kierkegaard as the great theorist of the Scene of Instruction, particularly in his brilliantly polemical text, the *Philo-*

sophical Fragments (1844). The title page of this short book asks the splendid triple question: "Is an historical point of departure possible for an eternal consciousness; how can such a point of departure have any other than a merely historical interest; is it possible to base an eternal happiness upon historical knowledge." Kierkegaard's intent is to refute Hegel by severely dividing Christianity from Idealist philosophy, but his triple question is perfectly applicable to the secular paradox of poetic incarnation and poetic influence. For the anxiety of influence stems from the ephebe's assertion of an eternal, divinating consciousness that nevertheless took its historical point of departure in an intra-textual encounter, and most crucially in the interpretative moment or act of misprision contained in that encounter. How indeed, the ephebe must wonder, can such a point of departure have more than merely historical rather than poetic interest? More anxiously, even, how is the strong poet's claim to poetic immortality (the only eternal happiness that is relevant) to be founded upon an encounter trapped belatedly in time?

Two sections of the *Fragments* are closest to the dilemmas of the poetic Scene of Instruction. These are the essay of the imagination called "The God as Teacher and Savior," and the ingenious chapter called "The Case of the Contemporary Disciple." The first is a concealed polemic against Strauss and Feuerbach as left-wing Hegelians, and the second is an overt polemic against Hegel himself. Against left-wing Hegelianism, Kierkegaard contrasts Socrates as a teacher with the Christ. Socrates and his student have nothing to teach one another, no *davhar* or word to bring forward, yet each provides the other with a means towards self-understanding. But the Christ understands himself without the aid of students, and his students are there only to receive his incommensurable love. Against Hegel, Kierkegaard separates history from Necessity, for Christian truth is not a human possession, as Hegelian Idealism would believe. The contemporary disciple of the God as teacher and savior "was not contemporary with the splendor, neither hearing nor seeing anything of it." There is no immediacy by which one can be a contemporary of a divinity; the paradox of the peculiarly Kierkegaardian variety of "repetition" is at work here, and by an exploration of such repetition we can displace Kierkegaard's polemical wit into a speculation upon the Scene of Instruction, and simultaneously expose again an inadequacy in Freud's account of the compulsion to repeat, and that compulsion's relation to origins.

Repetition, in Kierkegaard, goes back at least to theses XII and XIII of his Master of Arts dissertation, *The Concept of Irony* (1841). Thesis XII smacks at Hegel for defining irony while considering only the modern but not so much the ancient Socratic form. Thesis XIII, also directed against Hegel, is one of the founding apothegms for any study of poetic misprision:

> Irony is not so much apathy, divested of all tender emotions of the soul; instead, it is more like vexation over the fact that others also enjoy what it desires for itself.

True repetition, for Kierkegaard, is eternity, and so only true repetition can save one from the vexation of irony. But this is an eternity in time, "the daily bread which satisfies with benediction." Indeed, this is the center of Kierkegaard's vision, and necessarily also of *his* anxiety of influence in regard to his reviled precursor, Hegel, for Kierkegaard's "repetition" is a substitute trope for Hegel's trope of "mediation," the process of dialectic itself. Kierkegaard's dialectic, by being more internalized, is doomed to even more subjectivity, a limitation that Kierkegaard characteristically sought to represent as a philosophical advance. If repetition is primarily a dialectical re-affirmation of the continued possibility of becoming a Christian, then its aesthetic displacement would re-affirm dialectically the continued possibility of becoming a poet. No contemporary disciple of a great poet then could be truly his precursor's contemporary, for the splendor is necessarily *deferred*. It can be reached through the mediation of repetition, by a return to origins and the incommensurable Election-love that the Primal

Scene of Instruction can bestow, there at the point of origin. Poetic repetition repeats a Primal repression, a repression that is itself a fixation upon the precursor as teacher and savior, or on the poetic father as mortal god. The compulsion to repeat the precursor's patterns is not a movement beyond the pleasure principle to an inertia of poetic pre-incarnation, to a Blakean Beulah where no dispute can come, but rather is an attempt to recover the prestige of origins, the oral authority of a prior Instruction. Poetic repetition quests, despite itself, for the mediated vision of the fathers, since such mediation holds open the perpetual possibility of one's own sublimity, one's election to the realm of true Instructors.

What can be the use of this involved, six-phased notion of a Scene of Instruction, itself a belated or metaleptic preface to a six-fold scheme of revisionary ratios that serve as a typology of intra-textual poetic evasions? Beyond the Gnostic exuberance of his misplaced *inventio*, the quester after an antithetical criticism can offer a double defense of his enterprise. First, there is the polemical motive, phrased best by Geoffrey Hartman:

> . . . the concern with influence, now seeing a revival, is a humanistic attempt to save art from those who would eliminate mind in favor of structure or who would sink it into the mechanical operation of the spirit. To save it from both structuralist and spiritualist, in other words. For influence, *in art*, is always personal, seductive, perverse, imposing. . . .

One can expand Hartman's point by a juxtaposition of Nietzsche, patron saint of structuralist deconstruction, and Kenneth Burke— a confrontation managed by Burke in his first book, *Counterstatement*. First Nietzsche:

> What we find words for is that for which we no longer have use in our own hearts. There is always a kind of contempt in the act of speaking.

To which Burke replies:

Contempt, indeed, so far as the original emotion was concerned, but not contempt for the act of speaking.

The first use then of a Scene of Instruction is to remind us of the humanistic loss we sustain if we yield up the authority of oral tradition to the partisans of *writing*, to those like Derrida and Foucault who imply for all language what Goethe erroneously asserted for Homer's language, that language by itself writes the poems and thinks. The human writes, the human thinks, and always following after and defending against another human, however fantasized that human becomes in the strong imaginings of those who arrive later upon the scene.

Polemic never takes us far; at best it generates a disruptive force of speech against writing, against what Derrida calls the "aphoristic energy of writing and against the difference generally." Polemic can show us that the concept of "writing" is too overt and intentional a bulwark against the forces of continuity, against theology and logocentric tradition and, most self-defeatingly, against the concept of the book. The true use of a Scene of Instruction comes where true use must, as an aid to reading, an aid to the pragmatics of interpretation. I will close this chapter by juxtaposing two texts of Milton to one of Wordsworth, reading backwards up my categories of Instruction. Set *Tintern Abbey* against its most profound and anxiety-inducing ancestors, the invocations to Books III and VII of *Paradise Lost*. On the critical model of the Primal Scene of Instruction, a total interpretation of *Tintern Abbey* might proceed as follows. First, in what ways is *Tintern Abbey* a revision, a reading-by-misprision, of the Miltonic invocations? The answers will be found in the dance of substitutions, of one trope for another, one defense against another, one imagistic masking in evasion of another, that makes up the rhetoric that is *Tintern Abbey*'s. But this is only the start of a total reading. Mounting up our ladder of Instruction, we come to *lidrosh* or interpretation proper, and we can ask: what interpretation of Milton's invocations does *Tintern Abbey* make, both overtly and implicitly? We then may begin to notice aspects of Wordsworth's poem we scarcely saw before. There is the Hermit, meditating by a fire in a cave, who so strangely and suddenly enters at the conclusion of the first verse-paragraph of Wordsworth's poem. There is the blind man's eye, cut off from the "beauteous forms" of landscape, at the start of the next verse-paragraph. There is the vocabulary of presence and interfusion, of a creation overcoming all subject-and-object-dualisms, of the third verse-paragraph. There are the "genial spirits" that resist decay at the start of the fourth verse-paragraph and the reference to the poet's defense against "evil tongues" a few lines further on. All these testify to the surprising extent to which Wordsworth's poem is a defensive interpretation of the invocations to Books III and VII, and they give perhaps as much insight into Milton's texts as their presence gives opportunity for insight as to Wordsworth's less obvious preoccupations.

One more step up our scale, and we are led to ask the logophonic question: what is the Word (*davhar*) of his own, both as against and as related to the Word of Milton, that Wordsworth is compelled to bring forward in *Tintern Abbey?* The answer should illuminate the burden of vocation in Wordsworth's poem, and perhaps clarify the problematic of memory in the poem. Another move up the interpretative chain, and the contrast of rival inspirations should take us deep into the dark conflict in Wordsworth between the muse of Milton and the muse that is Nature. This hidden war is indeed between rival modes of Instruction, and it too would be seen more clearly against the background of a primal repressiveness.

A more difficult, indeed a Higher Criticism begins when we ask what kind of Covenant-love between the Milton of the invocations, and Wordsworth, is hinted at by *Tintern Abbey?* What does Wordsworth pledge to his precursor, and what does he expect to receive? Most difficult but also most fascinating is the final question, which returns us to the assimilative fixation in which any Primal Scene of Instruction must begin. What is the Election-love that is both offered by, and yet justifies, *Tintern Abbey* as a poem?

How does Wordsworth, for all his acute self-consciousness, his realization of his own belatedness, find the audacity to claim succession to Milton's authority and, even more crucially, to Milton's allusive yet wholly achieved sense of priority?

I conclude with a challenge, partly to those who see poetry as a performance of the Scene of Writing, and partly to those who follow the spiritualizing hermeneutics of anagogy and the *figura*. For these—both latest-model Structuralists and latest-model Spiritualists—are surprisingly alike in refusing to see the degree of revisionary compensation that psychically informs their work. Rousseau and Nietzsche, Blake and Emerson, despite all their differences, shared a blindness towards the canonical authorities they sought to invert or subvert. The Bible and Milton are not mocked, and even more vitally are not *contained by* their revisionists. Primal repression carried over into repetition yields the Sublime repression of belatedness or Romanticism, yet the fathers not only remain unaltered by the sons (except *in* the sons) but do not cease from altering their progeny. The last truth of the Primal Scene of Instruction is that purpose or aim—that is to say, meaning—cleaves more closely to origins the more intensely it strives to distance itself from origins.

4

The belatedness of strong poetry

What is the larger subject of which the study of poetic influence is only a part? Of what impulse is the revisionary impulse engendered? Who speaks, most grandly, for the isolate Selfhood?

>   . . . who saw
> When this creation was? remember'st thou
> Thy making, while the Maker gave thee being?
> We know no time when we were not as now;
> Know none before us, self-begot, self-rais'd
> By our own quick'ning power, when fatal course
> Had circl'd his full Orb, the birth mature
> Of this our native Heav'n, Ethereal Sons.
> Our puissance is our own, our own right hand
> Shall teach us highest deeds, by proof to try
> Who is our equal. . . .

Satan speaks; the impulse is that of self-begetting; the larger subject is precisely "quickening power." But take the power first at its most apparently sanctified, in Eckhart:

> I have said that there is one agent alone in the soul that is free. Sometimes I have called it the tabernacle of the Spirit. Other times I have called it the Light of the Spirit and again, a spark. Now I say that it is neither this nor that. It is something higher than this or that, as the sky is higher than the earth and I shall call it by a more aristocratic name than I have ever used before, even though it disowns my adulation and my name, being far

beyond both. It is free of all names and unconscious of any kind
of forms. It is at once pure and free, as God himself is, and like
him is perfect unity and uniformity, so that there is no possible
way to spy it out.

God blossoms and is verdant in this agent of which I speak,
with all the Godhead and spirit of God and there he begets his
only begotten Son as truly as if it were in himself. . . .

"In part the soul is like God," Eckhart adds, dangerously en-
croaching against the Protestant God's warning: "Be not too like
Me." The center is in Eckhart's insistence that: "There is some-
thing uncreated, something divine in the soul. . . ." In the Ameri-
can version, we can hear this true accent in Emerson, father of the
American Romantic Selfhood: "It is by yourself without ambas-
sador that God speaks to you," and "It is God in you that responds
to God without, or affirms his own words trembling on the lips of
another."

Quickening power comes when the Selfhood stands in its own
defense, the Selfhood being no outer man, but a sense of one's own
divinity, of being one's own only begotten son. This is the Self-
hood in its glory, *spheral man*, perfectly enclosed by a difficult
radiance. Is there a larger jeopardy to this radiance than the sense
of the Primal Scene? Here is a denial of such a sense, by a mind
of the greatest distinction:

> [The primal scene] often has the attractiveness of giving a sort
> of tragic pattern to one's life. It is all the repetition of the same
> pattern which was settled long ago. . . .
>
> There is of course the difficulty of determining what scene is
> the primal scene—whether it is the scene which the patient recog-
> nizes as such, or whether it is the one whose recollection effects
> the cure. . . .
>
> Analysis is likely to do harm. Because although one may dis-
> cover in the course of it various things about oneself, one must
> have a very strong and keen and persistent criticism in order to
> recognize and see through the mythology that is offered or im-
> posed on one. . . .

It is fair to remark that these are only notes of Wittgenstein in conversation, but as reported by a disciple. The fear of analytic harm here may be related to Rilke's celebrated complaint that analysis would have cost him his angels as well as his demons. The distinction made in the second quoted paragraph is palpably an evasion, and the emphasis upon the Primal Scene is revelatory not only of this philosopher's personal sorrows, but more crucially of his peculiar status as a great inventor, a strong poet of his discipline. The Primal Scene, for the philosopher *qua* philosopher in him, took place between Schopenhauer and the Muse of metaphysics. Wittgenstein, who together with his descendants clarified the enigmas of solipsism for our time, radiates the glory of the solipsist who taught that what the solipsist *means* (not what he says) is right.

Primal Scenes presumably induce a sort of vertigo in Selfhoods sufficiently spheral because they force a knowledge of the "no time" when indeed "we were not as now." What sublime sense of one's own being can survive the grotesquerie of confronting origins? The artist, as Nietzsche taught Yeats, is truly the antithetical man, with his personality set against his character, but there is nothing antithetical about the Primal Scene. Here, at least, what the solipsist *means* may not be right. The complaint of Wittgenstein against Freud—"a powerful mythology"—takes its poignance from the philosopher's sense that *this* power is not quickening, but reducing and even deadening, a terrible dualism though without an overt metaphysics.

A powerful mythology (Stanislaus Lec: "Myth is gossip grown old") does not form itself unless there is mental space to receive it, and the rationalized Romanticism of the Freudian mythology will not be cleared away soon enough to allow another Western story of origins in our time. Increasingly we can see the Cartesian dualism not as the Romantic adversary so much as another starting-point of Romantic mythology. Adam in Eden, Wallace Stevens said, was the father of Descartes, and now we can add that Descartes, as much as Milton, was the father of Wordsworth, for it was Descartes who so dangerously internalized the image of the quest for salvation. Caught in a ruined world, the pre-Cartesian quester sent forth his spirit to seek God's Son. After Descartes, the two realms of fallen and unfallen were joined, and rather than see nature raised to the Son, men brought the spirit down to the world of extension. Thought, Freud insisted, could be liberated from its sexual or dualistic past, by the rare person capable of true sublimation, but Descartes persuaded all who came after him otherwise, and it is difficult to believe that Freud persuaded even himself.

At the center of the Romantic vision is the beautiful lie of the Imagination, the only god. There is phantasmagoria and there is disciplined invention, and perhaps a third mode, hovering between the two, which makes us love poetry because we can find this middle mode nowhere else, but what is the Imagination unless it is the rhetorician's greatest triumph of self-deception? We cannot reduce the Imagination because it is the center of a powerful mythology and because we can never persuade ourselves again, as Hobbes so grandly did, that this portentous entity was once only gossip. Sense decays, and a phantom is born.

How high does the candle of the Imagination as God light the dark? Any phenomenology of religious experience properly begins with an empirical recognition of *power*, and even the strong Romantic Imagination is not capable of any power over things as they are. Things as they are explain themselves; power stands apart. Yet power once was the only true subject of poetry, in "Babylon the glory of kingdoms," where the poets sang only of heaven and hell. And power surely was Milton's true subject:

> Him the Almighty Power
> Hurl'd headlong flaming from th'Ethereal Sky
> With hideous ruin and combustion down
> To bottomless perdition. . . .

Milton's influence was one with his power, a power so barbaric as to justify Empson, Milton's best critic, when he compared it to

Benin sculpture. This power has something to do with the Christian religion, but rather more it stems from the exuberance of Milton's own selfhood. What do scholars mean when they call Milton *primarily* a Christian poet? As man, evidently he was Christian (of his own sect, a sect of one) but as poet he was a fierce Miltonist, and as much a son of himself as of God. If the Imagination, in poetry, speaks of itself, then it speaks of origins, of the archaic, of the primal, and above all of self-preservation. Vico is our best guide to the place of the Imagination, because he understood best this self-defining function of Imagination. Auerbach, writing on Vico's "magic formalism," gives a lucid summary: "The aim of primitive imagination, in his view, is not liberty, but, on the contrary, establishment of fixed limits, as a psychological and material protection against the chaos of the surrounding world." There is an Epicurean element in Vichian doctrine, as befits the intellectual tradition of Naples, which opposed Bruno to Aristotelian Scholasticism, and which accepted the Enlightened arguments of Bacon, Descartes and Hobbes. Vico, a Cartesian until he was twice-born at the age of forty, turned against Descartes on the principle that God alone knows all things, because he made all things. If you can know only what you have made, then if you know a text, what you know is the interpretation of it that you have made. Vico's imagination defended itself against the powerful Cartesian imagination by extending the Cartesian view of history to psychology, and thus swerving into a new view of history. Hobbes had said that history was "but experience, or authority, and not ratiocination." Descartes had deprecated whatever was of gradual maturation, denouncing both "our desires and our preceptors" and lamenting that "from birth" we had not our full-grown adult minds. Vico transcended both precursors by returning authority to our historical births, and by defining authority as poetic wisdom or the imagination. As the great instrument of self-preservation, the Vichian imagination is at once a composite of all Freud's "mechanisms of defense" and of all the tropes described by ancient rhetoricians. Eloquence is thus self-preservation through persuasion, and the imagination can do anything because self-preservation makes us giants and heroes and magical, primitive formalists again. Emerson is totally Vichian when he identifies rhetoric and reality, in his late essay "Poetry and Imagination":

> For the value of a trope is that the hearer is one: and indeed Nature itself is a vast trope, and all particular natures are tropes. As the bird alights on the bough, then plunges into the air again, so the thoughts of God pause but for a moment in any form. All thinking is analogizing, and it is the use of life to learn metonymy.

What Emerson is *not* saying is that we are in the dungeon of language. Lacan asserts that "it is the world of words that creates the world of things," and Jakobson, less figuratively, allows himself to insist that the poetry of grammar produces the grammar of poetry. Emerson, like all central poets, knows that the grammar of poetry produces the grammar of poetry, since poetry is a discursive and not a linguistic mode. Holmes remarked that "Emerson was eminently sane for an idealist," and such sanity is eminently useful now in current discussions of the arts of interpretation.

In Heidegger the thinking subject is subordinated to language, according to the principle that our Being is determined by our potentiality for discourse: "The intelligibility of something has always been articulated, even before there is any appropriate interpretation of it." Sapir independently phrased this contention less dogmatically by suggesting that "thought may be a natural domain apart from the artificial one of speech, but speech would seem to be the only road we know that leads to it." Against these views, which have become fundamental to much Structuralist criticism, a return to Vico and Emerson should demonstrate that *belatedness* or the fear of time's revenges is the true dungeon for the imagination, rather than the prison-house of language as posited by Nietzsche, Heidegger and their heirs.

What can the imagination defend us against except the preemptive force of another imagination? To originate anything in language we must resort to a trope, and that trope must defend us against a prior trope. Owen Barfield, in his essay "Poetic Diction and Legal Fiction," is in the line of Vico, Emerson and Coleridge when he observes that "repetition is inherent in the very meaning of the word 'meaning.'" To say and mean something new, we must use language, and must use it figuratively. Barfield cites Aristotle saying of metaphor that "it alone does not mean borrowing from someone else." On Barfield's view, increased knowledge of language, understanding "as fully as possible the relation between prediction and suggestion, between 'saying' and 'meaning,'" is the way out of the prison-house aspect of language.

Returning to Vico and to Emerson is to see that origins, poetic and human, not only rely upon tropes, but *are* tropes. Poetic meaning, despite the awesome interpretative self-confidence of both Vico and Emerson, is therefore radically indeterminate. Reading, despite all humanist traditions of education, is very nearly impossible, for every reader's relation to every poem is governed by a figuration of belatedness. Tropes or defenses (for here rhetoric and psychology are a virtual identity) are the "natural" language of the imagination in relation to all prior manifestations of imagination. A poet attempting to make this language new necessarily begins by an *arbitrary act of reading* that does not differ in kind from the act that *his* readers subsequently must perform upon him. In order to become a strong poet, the poet-reader begins with a trope or defense that *is* a misreading, or perhaps we might speak of the trope-as-misreading. A poet interpreting his precursor, and any strong subsequent interpreter reading either poet, must *falsify* by his reading. Though this falsification can be quite genuinely perverse or even ill-willed, it need not be, and usually is not. But it must be a falsification, because every strong reading insists that the meaning it finds is exclusive and accurate. Paul de Man, expounding Nietzsche's theory of rhetoric, defines Nietzsche's mode of misreading as an amalgam of the notions of the "will to power" and of "interpretation": "Both combine in the forceful reading that presents itself as absolutely true but can then, in its turn, be undermined. The will to power functions as the willful re-interpretation of all reality."

Nietzsche, though a highly self-conscious theorist of rhetoric (and of revisionism), is rightly presented by de Man as being not a special case, but rather a paradigm for our understanding of intra-textual encounters or, as I would term them, literary misprisions. In order for a reading (misreading) to be itself productive of other texts, such a reading is compelled to assert its uniqueness, its totality, its truth. Yet language *is* rhetoric, and intends to communicate opinion rather than truth, so that the "errors" of rhetoric are simply the same as its constituent tropes. Though one need not agree either with Nietzsche's overt irony in defense of art ("Art treats appearance as appearance; its aim is precisely *not* to deceive, it is therefore *true*") or with de Man's implicit irony that error cannot be distinguished from imagination, the insights of both theorists seem essential to any account of intra-poetic relationships.

Vico says of primal imagination that it was wholly corporeal and hence marvelously sublime, and so met the needs of a robust ignorance. Unfortunately, all of the poetry we know (including all the actual poetry that Vico knew) necessarily rises from a less corporeal and therefore less sublime imagination. Every poem we know begins as an encounter *between poems*. I am aware that poets and their readers prefer to believe otherwise, but acts, persons, and places, if they are to be handled by poems at all, must themselves be treated first as though they were already poems, or parts of poems. Contact, in a poem, means contact with another poem, even if that poem is called a deed, person, place or thing. What I mean by "influence" is the whole range of relationships between one poem and another, which means that my use of "influence" is itself a highly conscious trope, indeed a complex sixfold trope that intends to subsume six major tropes: irony, synecdoche, metonymy, hyperbole, metaphor, and metalepsis, and in just that ordering.

In her *Elizabethan and Metaphysical Imagery*, Rosamund Tuve remarked that "any trope departs in some tiny degree from the sensuous function toward what we should call, I suppose, suggestion; but what it suggests is an interpretation, not more and more empirical data however precise." What I offer through my six tropes are six interpretations of influence, six ways of reading/misreading intra-poetic relationships, which means six ways of reading a poem, six ways that intend to combine into a single scheme of complete interpretation, at once rhetorical, psychological, imagistic and historical, though this is an historicism that deliberately reduces to the interplay of personalities. But because my six tropes or ratios of revisionism are not tropes only, but also psychic defenses, what I call "influence" is a figuration for poetry itself; not as the relation of product to source, or effect to cause, but as the greater relation of latecomer poet to precursor, or of reader to text, or of poem to the imagination, or of the imagination to the totality of our lives.

If we consider "influence" as the trope of rhetorical irony that connects an earlier to a later poet ("irony" as figure of speech, not as figure of thought), then influence is a relation that means one thing about the intra-poetic situation while saying another. Influence is, in this phase, which I have termed *clinamen*, an initial error because nothing can be in its proper place. We might phrase this as a conscious state of rhetoricity, the poem's opening awareness that it *must be mis-read* because its signification has wandered already. An intolerable presence (the precursor's poem) has been voided, and the new poem starts in the *illusio* that this absence can deceive us into accepting a new presence. The dialectic of presence and absence becomes on a psychological basis the primary defense that Freud termed reaction-formation, the ego's prime protection against the id. A rhetorical irony is like the limitation of cramping or rigidity that serves to hinder the expression of contrary impulses while simultaneously making the counter-cathexis quite manifest.

After this initial contraction, influence as trope and as defense turns against itself, in a restituting movement. Rhetorically this substitution tends to be performed as a synecdoche, in which a more comprehensive term replaces a lesser representation. As the part yields to an antithetical whole, influence comes to mean a kind of belated completion, which I have called *tessera*. In Freudian terms, this ratio combines two related defenses, turning-against-the-self and reversal, respectively a turning of aggressive impulses inwards, and a fantasy in which the situation of reality is reversed so as to sustain negation or denial from any outward overthrow. In effect influence becomes a part, of which self-revisionism and self-rebegetting is the whole.

All restitutions or representations induce fresh anxieties, and the influence-process continues by a compensatory fresh limitation, for which the appropriate trope is metonymy and the parallel defenses are the allied triad of regression, undoing and isolation. This second limitation, more deeply self-wounding than irony, is the ratio I have termed *kenosis*. As a metonymy for influence, it conveys an emptying-out of a prior fullness of language, even as the irony of influence was the voiding or absenting of a presence. Influence as repetition is thus substituted for influence as genesis, or to adopt the linguistic trope, contiguity replaces resemblance, as the name or prime aspect of influence replaces its larger meanings. As a defense, *kenosis* isolates by removing instinctual impulses from their context while retaining them in consciousness, which means by removing the precursor from his context. The same process undoes by opposition what was done before; this is what forms the aspect of metonymy that makes it so difficult to distinguish from synecdoche. Most crucially, influence as a metonymy defends against itself by regression, by a return to earlier periods of supposed creativity when poetic experience seemed more an unmixed pleasure, and when the satisfactions of composition seemed more complete.

Influence conceived as an hyperbole takes us into the realms of Sublime representation, restituting for the emptyings-out of metonymy. The accent of excess here is allied to the defense of repression, for the high imageries of hyperbole conceal an unconsciously purposeful forgetting, or not becoming aware, of those internal impulses that tempt us towards gratifying objectionable instinctive demands. Hyperbole as the trope for influence seems to me the most important of my six ratios for High Romanticism, hyperbolical in its visions of the imagination, and so here the process of influence is identical with all belated versions of the Sublime.

Rhetoricians from Aristotle to our contemporaries, and moralists from Plato to Nietzsche and Freud, give the honor of greatest importance to the trope of metaphor, and its allied defense of sublimation, but here I judge us to be back in the mode of limitation rather than in representation, as this book will attempt to explain. As a trope for influence, metaphor transfers the name of influence to a series of inapplicable objects, in an *askesis* or work of sublimation that is itself a substitute gratification. This is an active defense, since under the influence of the ego, a substitute aim or object replaces the original impulse, on a basis of selective similarity. Influence as a metaphor for reading thus takes the place of a more primal, a more Vichian imagination of reading. Yet, despite the prestige of metaphor, it too is a trope of limitation. As Burke says, irony commits its user to a dialectic of presence and absence; metonymy compels a reduction from a fullness to an emptiness of language; metaphor yet more powerfully limits poetry by creating a perspectivism of inside against outside, another subject-object dualism to add further burdens for the imagination. Sublimation in life may be wisdom; in literature it courts defeat, since the acceptance it brings about in the self's sense of its own diminishment is also the acceptance of a precursor's survival as the inevitable form of the other, as a dualism that never again can be banished.

This book emphasizes influence as a sixth trope, a metalepsis or transumption of the process of reading (and writing) poems, a final ratio of revision that I have named *apophrades*, or the return of the precursors. Metalepsis, condemned by Quintilian as a trope good only for comedy, and still considered far-fetched by many

Renaissance theorists, acquired a new importance from Milton onwards, if the argument of Chapter 7 of this book proves to be correct. Metalepsis is defined and illustrated rather exhaustively in that chapter; here its relation to the defenses of introjection and projection requires emphasis. We can define metalepsis as the trope of a trope, the metonymic substitution of a word for a word already figurative. More broadly, a metalepsis or transumption is a scheme, frequently allusive, that refers the reader back to any previous figurative scheme. The related defenses are clearly introjection, the incorporation of an object or instinct so as to overcome it, and projection, the outward attribution of prohibited instincts or objects to an other. Influence as a metalepsis for reading tends to be either a projection and distancing of the future and so an introjection of the past, by substituting late words for early words in previous tropes, or else more often a distancing and projection of the past and an introjection of the future, by substituting early words for late words in a precursor's tropes. Either way the present vanishes and the dead return, by a reversal, to be triumphed over by the living.

What is the use of this sixfold trope for the act of reading? Why talk of influence except in the traditional terms of source-study? Begin by realizing again that, as de Man says, all criticism is a metaphor for the act of reading. The proposal then is to enrich criticism by finding a more comprehensive and suggestive trope for the act of interpretation, a trope antithetical not only to all other tropes but to itself in particular. If all tropes are defenses against other tropes, then the use of influence as a composite trope for interpretation may be that it will defend us against itself. Perhaps, at this belated time, interpretation has become the reader's defense. Must we indeed interpret as a way of gaining power over the text? Does interpretation now begin with the reader's anxiety? Is the reader now the vulnerable and belated one, fearful that he can only block his own individuating by his reading? If these questions are to be answerable, we need to be less idealistic about interpretation than we generally are.

The interpretation of a poem necessarily is always interpretation of that poem's interpretation of other poems. When I said that once, in a lecture on the revisionary ratio of *askesis,* or influence as a metaphor for reading, a poet of real achievement rose from the audience to protest that *his* poems were not about Yeats but about life, his own life. To which I replied by asking where his stance, as poet, in relation to life originated, and by what means he had learned to define it so as to justify his writing a poem at all. But I should also have asked what he meant when he said his poems were "about" something, that this or that was their "subject." The root meaning of "about" is to be on the outside of something, and a poem "about" life truly is on the outside of life. To study what poems are about is to interpret their outside relationships. A "subject" is indeed under something else, and a poem's subject thus subjects the poem.

To interpret a poem, necessarily you interpret its difference from other poems. Such difference, where it vitally creates meaning, is a family difference, by which one poem expiates for another. Since meaning, as difference, rhetorically depends upon troping, we can conclude that tropes are defenses, and what they defend poems against are tropes in other poems, or even earlier tropes in the very same poems. Tropes and poems can relate to life, but only after first relating to other figurations. Peirce is the theoretician who best defines both the anxiety of influence and the intra-textual necessities of meaning that rise from it:

> If there are some indications that something greatly for my interest, and which I have anticipated would happen, may not happen; and if, after weighing probabilities, and inventing safeguards, and straining for further information, I find myself unable to come to any fixed conclusion in reference to the future, in the place of that intellectual hypothetic influence which I seek, the feeling of *anxiety* arises.

Nietzsche, who knew that all we had to interpret was already an interpretation, advised us to seek the dialectic of every interpretation in the interpreter. Peirce urges an even deeper knowledge of the anteriority of every cognition, let alone every text:

> . . . We know of no power by which an intuition could be known. For, as the cognition is beginning, and therefore in a state of change, at only the first instant would it be intuition. And, therefore, the apprehension of it must take place in no time and be an event occupying no time. Besides, all the cognitive faculties we know of are relative, and consequently their products are relations. But the cognition of a relation is determined by previous cognitions. No cognition not determined by a previous cognition, then, can be known. It does not exist, then, first, because it is absolutely incognizable, and second, because a cognition only exists so far as it is known.

If we transpose Peirce's insights into more strictly literary terms, while keeping his sense that language is the problematic (or part of it, the larger part being time), we can state a basic principle of antithetical interpretation. *All interpretation depends upon the antithetical relation between meanings, and not on the supposed relation between a text and its meaning.* If no "meaning" of a "reading" intervenes between a text and yourself, then you start (even involuntarily) by making the text *read itself.* You are compelled to treat it as an interpretation of itself, but pragmatically this makes you expose the relation between its meaning and the meaning of other texts. As the language of a poet is his stance, his relation to the language of poetry, you therefore measure his stance in regard to his precursors' stance.

Such measurement is a calibration of the play of substitutions, of tropes and defenses, images and arguments, passions and ideas, all of which make up every poet's battle to accomplish a reversal in which his lateness will become a strength rather than a weakness. Paul de Man would insist that in the study of this struggle for reversal, the linguistic model usurps the psychological one because language is a substitute system responsive to the will, but the psyche is not. But that is to interpret the term "influence" as one trope only, as a metaphor that transforms encounters between linguistic structures into diachronic narratives. Influence would thus be reduced to semantic tension, to an interplay between literal and figurative meanings. As the sixfold, composite trope outlined above, influence remains subject-centered, a person-to-person relationship, not to be reduced to the problematic of language. From the viewpoint of criticism, a trope is just as much a concealed mechanism of defense, as a defense is a concealed trope. The burden for readers remains that poetry, despite all its protests, continues to be a discursive mode, whose structures evade the language that would confine them.

The affliction of belatedness, as I have begun to recognize, is a recurrent malaise of Western consciousness, and I would now recant my previous emphasis on the anxiety of influence as a Post-Enlightenment phenomenon. William Arrowsmith has observed, with a certain mordant splendor, that Euripides can be considered a misprision of Aeschylus, and Dr. Samuel Johnson with equally elegant gloom found Virgil to be deformed by his anxieties about Homer. Though I would now assert only a difference in degree, rather than in kind, for influence-anxieties from Milton on, this is nevertheless a true difference for reading, and for the pragmatics of interpretation. We can distinguish poetic belatedness from the general sense of cultural undervaluation that Bacon battled against in Renaissance England. Bacon insisted that the ancients were the true moderns, and the moderns the true ancients, because those who arrived later knew more, even if they were of lesser genius:

> . . . The children of time do take after the nature and malice of the father. For as he devoureth his children, so one of them seeketh to devour and suppress the other, while antiquity envieth there should be new additions, and novelty cannot be content to add but it must deface. Surely the advice of the prophet is the true direction in this matter, *Stand in the old ways, and see which is the straight and good path, and walk in that.* Antiquity deserveth that reverence, that men should make a stand thereupon, and discover what is the best way, but when the discovery is

well taken, then to make progression. And to speak truly, *The antiquity of time is the youth of the world*. These times are the ancient times, when the world is ancient, and not those which we account ancient *ordine retrogrado*, by a computation backward from ourselves.

Yet the post-Miltonic situation for a poet could not be mended by a Baconian reasoned optimism. Milton, as Chapter 7 will try to demonstrate, triumphed over his precursors by developing a "transumptive" mode of allusion, but Milton himself could not be reversed by his followers. If his preternatural strength, his uncanny blend of cultural lateness and poetic earliness, was partly his admirers' creation, that mystification was not less strong for being self-imposed. Milton, not Shakespeare or Spenser, became a kind of Gnostic father-figure for subsequent poetry written in English. Shakespeare and Spenser alike appear to leave some room for the female in all creativity, but Milton fundamentally gives us Milton's God and the Christ who rides the Chariot of Paternal Deity, the same Chariot in which Gray, Blake, and Keats were more inclined to see Milton himself as rider.

Belatedness is certainly the Satanic predicament in Milton, and as certainly it was the predicament in which Milton did not deign to find himself. Self-presence Milton appears to treat as almost his birthright, his personal version of Christian Liberty. Yet it seems clear that from the 1740's on, poets felt a sense of trespass, however obscure, when they asserted self-presence by daring to come into Milton's presence, as poets in their own right. Geoffrey Hartman has written illuminatingly on the post-Miltonic poet's "deed" of self-presence, stressing the uniqueness of Milton's "decisive textual and imaginative pressure on English poetry," but also stating a preference for a phenomenological over a psychoanalytic view of self-presence. What Freud termed a "memorable and criminal deed," the primal history scene of *Totem and Taboo*, is to be replaced by the necessary trespass of becoming conscious of otherness, as such, or simply of the effort of consciousness to "appear."

Hartman, writing of Keats's Apollo in the fragmentary third book of *Hyperion*, says of him that "to bring his identity to light means to bear a father god out of himself." Unfortunately, Keats could not realize this program. *Hyperion* breaks off with this light-bearing, and *The Fall of Hyperion*, though the greater of the two fragments, is also the more anxiety-ridden, as Hartman notes, for no poem in the language is more beautifully haunted by its own conscious belatedness.

The use of any psychopoetics is to find a way back to an enrichment of rhetorical criticism, which is one of the purposes of this book. Yet I do not propose a yielding to any purely rhetorical criticism, however imported, however newfangled, any more than I would yield the burden of self-presence to descriptive rather than analytic accounts of consciousness. A full critical awareness of the phenomenon of belatedness and the resultant misprision worked by revisionism might lead to a kind of criticism we rarely possess, even in contemporaries like Wilson Knight, Burke, and Empson, who seem to me the largest and most authentic modern heirs of Coleridge, Hazlitt, Ruskin, Emerson and Pater. Criticism is in danger of being over-spiritualized by the heirs of Auerbach and by Northrop Frye, and of being excessively despiritualized by the followers of the school of Deconstruction, the heirs of Nietzsche, among whom Derrida, de Man, Hillis Miller are most distinguished. Figural interpretation has a compensatory and self-serving element in its too-certain assumption that later texts can "fulfill" earlier ones, just as archetypal interpretation too readily posits a shared generosity of spirit as the basis for great poetry. Yet the recent achievements of a de-idealizing criticism seem to rely both upon too narrow a canon of texts, and upon only parts of texts, where intra-textual differences tend to cluster or even protrude. Structuralist criticism, even in its latest and most refined model, commits itself to an antimimetic theory in which what Derrida calls "freeplay" seems the inevitably dominant concept, one in which every trope or semiotic turn is, as Hartman says, a kind of free fall. My own experience as a reader is that poets differentiate themselves into strength by troping or turning from the presence of other poets. Greatness results from a refusal to separate origins from aims. The father is met in combat, and fought to at least a stand-off, if not quite to a separate peace. The burden for representation thus becomes supermimetic rather than antimimetic, which means that interpretation too must assume the experiential sorrows of a supermimesis. I hope, by urging a more antithetical criticism, one that constantly sets poet against poet, to persuade the reader that he too must take on his share of the poet's own agon, so that the reader also may make of his own belatedness a strength rather than an affliction.

Part II
THE MAP

5

The map of misprision

I don't know whether it happens with others as with me; but
when I hear our architects puffing themselves out with those
big words like pilasters, architraves, cornices, Corinthian and
Doric work, and such-like jargon, I cannot keep my imagination
from immediately seizing on the palace of Apollidon; and in
reality I find that these are the paltry parts of my kitchen door.
When you hear people talk about metonymy, metaphor, alle-
gory, and other such names in grammar, doesn't it seem that
they mean some rare and exotic form of language? They are
terms that apply to the babble of your chambermaid.
        Montaigne, Of the Vanity of Words *(Frame version)*

The New Testament purports to "fulfill" the Old. Blake came, he
sometimes thought, to "correct" Milton. Eduard Bernstein,
founder of the modern sense of "revisionism," anticipated many
after him by supposedly seeking both to fulfill and to correct Marx,
a double quest since undertaken with respect to Freud by Jung and
many heresiarchs after him. All revisionists, however irreligious, are
anagogists, though frequently shallow in their anagogy. Spiritual
uplift too frequently is exposed as the drive towards power over
the precursors, a drive fixed in its origins and wholly arbitrary in its
aims. Nietzsche's critique of interpretation is both a de-mystification
of revisionism and another self-serving instance of revisionism, ris-
ing in Nietzsche out of his hatred of the perniciousness of his own
belatedness.

DIALECTIC OF REVISIONISM	IMAGES IN THE POEM	RHETORICAL TROPE	PSYCHIC DEFENSE	REVISIONARY RATIO
Limitation	Presence and Absence	Irony	Reaction-Formation	Clinamen
Substitution	↕	↕	↕	↕
Representation	Part for Whole or Whole for Part	Synecdoche	Turning against the self. Reversal	Tessera
Limitation	Fullness and Emptiness	Metonymy	Undoing, Isolation, Regression	Kenosis
Substitution	↕	↕	↕	↕
Representation	High and Low	Hyperbole, Litotes	Repression	Daemon-ization
Limitation	Inside and Outside	Metaphor	Sublimation	Askesis
Substitution	↕	↕	↕	↕
Representation	Early and Late	Metalepsis	Introjection, Projection	Apophrades

After Nietzsche and Freud, it is not possible to return wholly to a mode of interpretation that seeks to *restore* meanings to texts. Yet even the subtlest of contemporary Nietzschean "deconstructors" of texts must *reduce* those texts in a detour or flight from psychology and history. Nothing prevents a reader with my preferences from resolving all linguistic elements in a literary text into history, and similarly tracing all semantic elements in literary discourse to problems of psychology. A semiological enigma, however prized, is generally an elaborate evasion of the inevitable discursiveness of a literary text. Latecomer fictions must know themselves to be fictions, and perhaps any Greek fiction knew itself as such; but are we to say that the Bible knows itself as fiction? Deconstructive readings clear away illusions in texts that allow for particular illusions, but what *are* illusions in texts that turn wholly on regathering meanings or restoring the reader to some vision that such texts require of him?

"Interpretation" once meant "translation," and essentially still does. Freud compares dream-analysis to translation between languages. We can prefer Freud as a clearer-away of illusions to his chief competitor, Jung, who offers himself as a restorer of primal meanings but discredits almost all possibility of such restoration; but we will remain uneasy at the Freudian reductiveness, and wonder if another mode of dream-interpretation might yet emerge out of a more advanced study of poetry. And we have discovered no way as yet to evade the insights of Nietzsche, which are more dangerously far-reaching even than those of Freud, since Freud would not have told us that rational thought *is* only interpretation according to a scheme we cannot throw off. Yet Nietzsche's "perspectivism," which is all he can offer us as alternative to Western metaphysics, is a labyrinth more pragmatically illusive than the illusions he would dispel. One need not be religious in any sense or intention, or inclined to any degree of theosophy or occult speculation, still to conclude that meaning, whether of poems or of dreams, of any text, is excessively impoverished by a Nietzsche-inspired deconstruction, however scrupulous. Poems and dreams alike may *remind* us of what consciously we never have known, or think we never have known, or they make us *recall* kinds-of-knowing we thought no longer possible for us. Such tokens are not merely illusions to be dissolved by an attack even as thoroughgoing as Nietzsche's, which would end reminiscence or any study of the nostalgias by deconstructing the thinking subject itself, by dissipating the ego into a "rendezvous of persons." Blake, Balzac, Browning are among the nineteenth-century giants who in their work exemplified such a deconstruction of the ego more strikingly than Nietzsche did, yet all of them finally *interpreted* more in the mode of recollecting than of demystifying meaning. And what they recollected (among much else) were all the intervening stages between the sentient and the non-sentient world, between consciousness and the object, that had vanished from most post-Cartesian texts.

At issue is the evaluation of consciousness, since to Nietzsche and to Freud consciousness is, at best, a mask, yet to Blake and Browning (and Emerson) it need not be false but can prophesy the truth. Pragmatically, Nietzsche and Freud confound themselves, for their mutual aim is to intensify and to expand consciousness. We need to begin farther back than even Romantic tradition goes, in order to find a point of origin primordial enough to let us consider a history of the relations between Western self-consciousness and the spirit of revisionism.

The problem of originality, in Western conceptualization, is generally studied by starting from Plato. Thus Lovejoy began *The Great Chain of Being* by distinguishing two gods, both evidently Plato's, the Good of the *Philebus*, and the creative Demiurgus of the *Timaeus*, the first god "other-worldly" and the second "this-worldly." "The Good differs in its nature from everything else in that the being who possesses it always and in all respects has the most perfect sufficiency and is never in need of any other thing" [*Philebus*, 6oc]. This contrasts to a god who "was good, and in one that is good no envy of anything else ever arises. Being devoid of envy, then, he desired that everything should be so far as possible like himself" [*Timaeus*, 29]. Plato made these contrasting gods into what Lovejoy called: "Two-Gods-in-One, a divine completion which was yet *not* complete in itself, since it could not be itself without the existence of beings other than itself and inherently incomplete." In Neoplatonism and in medieval Christianity, as Lovejoy proceeded to demonstrate, this double-god continued to develop as "a conflict between two irreconcilable conceptions of the good." Man was to be assimilated, ultimately, to God, the assimilation primarily conceived as *imitation*. But to which god, or aspect of God? Was the precursor a god of "unity, self-sufficiency, and quietude" or a god of "diversity, self-transcendence, and fecundity?"

I offer this formula: in all precursor-ephebe relations of the Post-Enlightenment, imitation of the precursor takes as its paradigm the burden of imitating a double-god, for these two-gods-in-one are still present in Milton's God. Milton himself, to Collins or to Gray or even to Blake, offers the opposing aspects of a being so unified, self-sufficient and given to quietude *as to need no successors*, and yet also of a being so diverse, self-transcendent and fecund *as to compel generous imitation*. Milton, as sacred being or mortal god, radiates irreconcilable forms of the good. To those who would inherit from him, Milton's every act of limitation shows forth as a powerful representation, and Milton's every representation acts as a further limitation. Like Luria's *En Soph*, Milton compels his followers to make of their creative strivings a series of continual acts of restitution.

In the Introduction, I sketched a displacement of the Lurianic dialectics of creation into the aesthetic triad of limitation, substitution, representation. I suggest now that this dialectic be expanded into a map of misprision, a charting of *how meaning is produced* in Post-Enlightenment strong poetry by the substitutive interplay of figures and of images, by the language strong poets use in defense against, and response to, the language of prior strong poets. If I am to use Luria's story of creation as a revisionary paradigm, then I need to make a distinction between two kinds of tropes, a distinction not sanctioned by rhetoric ancient or modern;

though Kenneth Burke, in my reading of him, provides much of the basis for a division between *tropes of limitation* and *tropes of representation*. Similarly I need to make a distinction between two kinds of psychic defenses, and find no basis in psychoanalytic theory to aid me here, in what becomes my own revisionism in regard to Freud. Just as I wish to suggest that the series irony, metonymy, metaphor are tropes of limitation, and the series synecdoche, hyperbole, metalepsis are tropes of representation, so also I propose that the defenses fall into two antithetical series. The *defenses of limitation* are: reaction-formation; then the triad of undoing, isolating, regressing; and lastly sublimation. The *defenses of representation* are: first the duo of turning-against-the-self and reversal; next repression; lastly, the duo of introjection and projection. But here I must return to *The Anxiety of Influence* to explain why I employ the analogues of tropes and defenses as interchangeable forms of what I have called "revisionary ratios." As I am returning to the origins of this enterprise, I begin by asking fundamental questions: What is a rhetorical trope, what is a psychic defense, and what is the value of analogizing them? A practical criticism attempting to be antithetical needs to approach the antithetical in both its meanings. There is the antithetical as the counter-placing of rival ideas in balanced or parallel structures, phrases, words, and there is also the antithetical as the anti-natural, or the "imaginative" opposed to the natural. The first is the antithetical of Freud, in his investigation of "primal words"; the second is the antithetical of Nietzsche, as developed by Yeats in *Per Amica Silentia Lunae*, where he insists that "the other self, the anti-self or the antithetical self, as one may choose to name it, comes but to those who are no longer deceived, whose passion is reality." Freud's *rhetorical* meaning of antithetical is transposed by him from tropes to mechanisms (as he lamentably called them) of defense. Nietzsche's *psychological* meaning of antithetical is transposed by him (and then by Yeats) from defenses to tropes. An antithetical practical criticism must begin with the analogical principle that tropes and defenses are interchangeable when they appear *in poems*, where after all both appear only as images. What I have called "revisionary ratios" are tropes and psychic defenses, both and either, and are manifested in poetic imagery. A rhetorical critic can regard a defense as a concealed trope. A psychoanalytic interpreter can regard a trope as a concealed defense. An antithetical critic will learn to use both in turn, relying upon the substitution of analogues as being one with the poetic process itself.

Arbitrarily, I will begin with defenses, and then pass on to tropes, but with a brief digression first on the necessities of analogy. I grant that my method is precariously assimilative, and that my transfers from Freudian theory to poetry may seem curiously literal. But I seek to take back from Freud precisely what he himself took from the poets (or from Schopenhauer and Nietzsche, who themselves had taken it from the poets). This is what Freud called *Bedeutungswandel*, which Hartman translates as either "tropism of meaning" or "wandering signification." Since *Deutung* here means "interpretation" of latent meaning, it seems clear that such interpretation largely reveals modes of defensive conflict or of contrary tropes, with the purpose of uncovering the world of the *wish*. Rieff defends Freud's use of an analogical method as being consistent with the analogical nature of his data, for his data are all images, starting with the self. Consciously and proudly a dualist, Freud nevertheless overcame the dumbfoundering abyss between subject and object by his own revision of Schopenhauer, swerving away from his precursor's grand hyperbole of the Unconscious. Deidealizing Schopenhauer meant a return to Empedocles, to a dialectic of love and hate, and to a darker view of instinct, as the primal reality, than supposedly any later philosopher had given. Yet Freud's revision of Schopenhauer is a thinking-by-synecdoche, which is to say by means of the ratio of *tessera* or antithetical completion. Rieff invokes the synecdochal relation of microcosm-to-macrocosm to summarize the Freudian theory of the instincts: "The pleasures, too, were instincts, inserting themselves between the original inorganic state and its prompt reinstatement after matter has once come alive. Life was the absence of a perfect equilibrium of the instincts, and death a seeking after that perfection." It was from this part-whole representation that Ferenczi departed in *his* great revisionism in *Thalassa*, a masterpiece of *kenosis* or metonymic regression-to-origins. Freud and Ferenczi alike were relying upon the "wandering signification" of the poets in their visions of origins, and to this day it is more clarifying to explain Freud and Ferenczi by way of Whitman or Hart Crane in their oceanic longings, than it is to fix the "tropism of meaning" in Whitman or Crane by recourse to Freud and Ferenczi.

To recapture antithetical thinking for criticism we need to begin with an analogical formula that will hold together both the trope and the psychic defense within the poetic image. The formula I would venture I derive, by implication, from *Beyond the Pleasure Principle* and from *Thalassa*.

Freud was in his middle sixties when he wrote *Beyond the Pleasure Principle* and so inaugurated the great phase of his work that is dominated by the ratio of *apophrades*, the return of the precursors —Empedocles, Schopenhauer, Nietzsche—in colors not their own, in colors of Freud's own choosing. The first page of the book asserts that "priority and originality are not among the aims that psycho-analytic work sets itself," which we may take as the characteristic evasion to be expected from this strongest of modern poets. From the perspective of literary criticism, Freud's great advance here is in his theory of the relation between anxiety and defense. Anxiety is defined as "a particular state of expecting danger or preparing for it, even though it may be an unknown one." This anxiety is impossible to distinguish from defense, for such anxiety is itself a shield against every provocation from otherness. Indeed, such anxiety itself has priority; it does not exist under the reign of the pleasure principle. Prompted by this realization, Freud revises himself drastically, and tells us that certain dreams (in traumatic neurosis) are *not* wish-fulfillments, after all: "These dreams are endeavoring to master the stimulus retrospectively, by developing the anxiety whose omission was the cause of the traumatic neurosis." Repetition-compulsions, whether in dreams, desires, or acts, are defenses against anteriority, and are quite close, rhetorically, to metonymic reductions. As undoings, they quest to return to "an earlier state of things." In Freud's most audacious hypothesis, which is a Sublime hyperbole or triumph of repression, this quest is given the extraordinary oxymoronic name of the "death instinct": *"the aim of all life is death"* and *"inanimate things existed before living ones."* Finally, the formulation is perfected in: "An organism wishes to die only in its own fashion."

Presumably any poet wishes to end *as a poet*, if at all, only in his own fashion. Perhaps we can say that a man, even as a man, is capable of wishing to die, but by definition no poet, *as poet*, can wish to die, for that negates poethood. If death ultimately represents the earlier state of things, then it also represents the earlier state of meaning, or pure anteriority; that is to say, repetition of the literal, or literal meaning. Death is therefore a kind of literal meaning, or from the standpoint of poetry, *literal meaning is a kind of death. Defenses can be said to trope against death, rather in the same sense that tropes can be said to defend against literal meaning,* which is the antithetical formula for which we have been questing.

Ferenczi, in *Thalassa*, says that "one might quite properly speak of a condensed recapitulation of sexual development as taking place in each individual sex act." Similarly one might speak of all the revisionary ratios (defenses or tropes or the phenomenal maskings of both in images) following one another in truly central, very strong poems. Ferenczi sees the sex act as an attempt to "return to the state of rest enjoyed before birth." Analogously, we can see the poem as an attempt to return to pure anteriority at the same time that it ambivalently tropes against anteriority. Towards the close of *Thalassa*, Ferenczi cites Nietzsche's polemic against origins, with its refusal to distinguish between organic and inorganic matter. From this contention, Ferenczi comes to his version of a catastrophe-theory of creation, akin to Lurianic speculation:

> . . . to drop once and for all the question of the beginning and end of life, and conceive the whole inorganic and organic world as a perpetual oscillating between the will to live and the will to die in which an absolute hegemony on the part either of life or

of death is never attained . . . it seems as though life had always
to end catastrophically, even as it began, in birth, with a catas-
trophe. . . .

I would suggest that Ferenczi, like the Freud of *Beyond the
Pleasure Principle,* is talking in *Thalassa* about poems rather than
about people, or at least that his insights work better for poems
than for people. Beyond the pleasures of poetry lies the maternal
womb of language out of which poems arise, the literal meaning
that poems both evade and desperately seek.

I return to my earlier questions: what is a defense, and what is
a trope? Freud's term is *Abwehrmechanismen,* but his categories
are closer both to Lurianic hypostases and to rhetorical tropes than
to mechanisms; and we can dismiss the crudity of "mechanisms,"
once for all, as a now-tiresome bow to the supposed purities of a
rigorously "scientific" kind of observation. A defense then is a psy-
chic operation or process directed against *change,* change that
might disturb the ego as a stable entity. Defense is set against in-
ternal movements from the id, movements that must appear as
representations (desires, fantasies, wishes, memories). But though
a defense is intended to turn the ego away from meeting objection-
able internal demands, pragmatically a defense tends to turn or
trope from or against *another defense* (just as a trope tends to de-
fend against another trope).

Anna Freud is the classic expounder of the Freudian defenses,
and I follow her here in accepting ten defenses as basic. But just as
tropes blend into one another, so defenses are difficult to keep
apart. Since I have posited six revisionary ratios, and since in my
last chapter I have seen these ratios as being six tropes for the in-
fluence-process, I need six primary defenses also, and consequently
am happy to observe that Anna Freud's categories reduce very
neatly into six kinds of defense. Her triad of undoing, isolation and
regression are closely allied, and her duo of introjection and projec-
tion are uneasily allied as near-contraries; while her duo of turning-
against-the-self and reversal-into-the-opposite are quite difficult to

distinguish. It is at this point that I ask my reader to glance at my Map of Misprision, on page 84.

It will be seen that, following my Lurianic model, I classify certain tropes, defenses and images as being those of Limitation, and their matching partners as being more largely those of Representation, with the process of Substitution as the perpetual generator of the interplay between them. The discussion following is intended to justify these apparently arbitrary distinctions. But first I need to justify my direct association of particular tropes with particular defenses, and both with particular kinds of images. I need therefore first to re-define a trope, and then to re-define in turn my own six revisionary ratios through defining the common features that ally each grouping of tropes, defenses and images, and then to explain the sequence of my ordering of the ratios in the structures of poems.

A trope traditionally is defined as Quintilian's *figura*, though Quintilian distinguishes tropes from figures, tropes being the narrower concept. A trope is a word or phrase used in some way that is not literal; a figure is any kind of discourse departing from common usage. Tropes substitute words for other words, but figures need not depart from normal meaning. This distinction between tropes and figures is not a useful one, and Quintilian himself gets confused in a few places. Auerbach observes that "in later usage *figura* is generally regarded as the higher concept, including trope, so that any unliteral or indirect form of expression is said to be figurative." To re-define, let me say that a trope is *a willing error*, a turn from literal meaning in which a word or phrase is used in an improper sense, wandering from its rightful place. A trope is therefore a kind of falsification, because every trope (like every defense, which is similarly a falsification) is necessarily an interpretation, and so a mistaking. Put another way, a trope resembles those errors about life that Nietzsche says are necessary for life. De Man, expounding Nietzsche's theory of rhetoric, speaks of all causal fictions as being cumulative errors, because all causal fictions are reversible. Influence, for de Man as for Nietzsche, is such a causal fiction, but I myself see influence as a trope-of-tropes, an apotropaic or warding-off sixfold trope that surmounts its own errors eventually by recognizing itself as the figure of a figure.

A trope as I define it is again, deliberately, more Vichian than Nietzschean. Vico's poetic logic charmingly associates tropes with "poetic monsters and metamorphoses," necessary errors that "arose from a necessity of this first human nature, its inability to abstract forms or properties from subjects. By their logic they had to put subjects together in order to put their forms together, or to destroy a subject in order to separate its primary form from the contrary form which had been imposed upon it." Vico thus sees figures as defenses against any *given* that challenged "this first human nature," that interfered with the literalizing divination that he sees as the essence of the poetic urge.

Tropes then are necessary errors about language, defending ultimately against the deathly dangers of literal meaning, and more immediately against all other tropes that intervene between literal meaning and the fresh opening to discourse. Vico says that all tropes reduce to four: irony, metonymy, metaphor and synecdoche, which agrees with Kenneth Burke's analysis of what he calls "the Four Master Tropes" in an appendix to his *A Grammar of Motives.* I will follow both Vico and Burke in my own analysis, except that I will add two more tropes—hyperbole and metalepsis—to the class of master tropes that govern Post-Enlightenment poetry, following Nietzsche and de Man in needing two more tropes of representation to go beyond synecdoche in accounting for Romantic representations.

Burke associates irony with dialectic, metonymy with reduction, metaphor with perspective, and synecdoche with representation. Hyperbole and metalepsis I add as progressively more blinded or broken representation, where "blinding" or "breaking" is meant to suggest the Lurianic breaking-of-the-vessels or scattering-of-the-light which I have carried over into the poetic realm as substitution. As tropes of contraction or limitation, irony withdraws meaning through a dialectical interplay of presence and absence; metonymy reduces meaning through an emptying-out that is a kind of reification; metaphor curtails meaning through the endless perspectivizing of dualism, of inside-outside dichotomies. As tropes of restitution or representation, synecdoche enlarges from part to whole; hyperbole heightens; metalepsis overcomes temporality by a substitution of earliness for lateness. This too-rapid summary should be clarified by what follows.

I will follow the order of my own revisionary ratios from *The Anxiety of Influence* because their movement is founded both on the Lurianic model of the myth of creation (though I did not know this consciously when they came to me) and also on the model of the Wordsworthian crisis-poem, which is the paradigm for the modern lyric. I take the term "ratio" from several sources. Mathematically it means the relation between two similar quantities as determined by the number of times one contains the other. In monetary science, it is the quantitative relation in which one metal stands to another in respect to their value as money. Yet it retains its meaning of "thought," and I suspect I chose it initially because of Blake, who uses it scornfully. Hartman observes that Blake associates "ratio" with Newtonianism, and uses it to mean a "reductive or uncreative relation between two or more terms of similar magnitude." My revisionary ratios are relations between unequal terms, because the later poet always magnifies the precursor in the very act of falsifying ("interpreting") him. Hartman acutely points out that "fearful symmetry" in *The Tyger* should be read as meaning "fearful ratio," since *The Tyger*'s speaker is the ephebe and the Tyger's maker the precursor. The Tyger, as Hartman suggests, is thus a Spectre or Covering Cherub, imposed by the latecomer imagination upon itself.

It is against such a spectral image or blocking agent (call it creative anxiety) that the ratios of revision work, and I see now (as I could not earlier) that they work in matched or dialectical pairs—

clinamen/tessera; kenosis/daemonization; askesis/apophrades—
with each pair following the Lurianic pattern of limitation/substi-
tution/representation. I see also that all three pairs can be at work
in really comprehensive and ambitious poems, however long or
short. Indeed, I propose that the succession and alternation of the
three pairs of ratios form the pattern of what has been the central
tradition of the greater modern lyric, from its ancestors in Spenser's
Prothalamion and Milton's *Lycidas* on through its major establish-
ment in the Coleridge-Wordsworthian crisis lyric, with the crucial
descendants in the most famous shorter poems of Shelley, Keats,
Tennyson, Browning, Whitman, Dickinson, Yeats, and Stevens
down to the best poems being written today. Whatever their for-
mal divisions into stanzas, a remarkable number of central poems
in Romantic tradition divide argumentatively and imagistically
into three parts, very much on the model of the *Intimations* Ode.
These are: first, an initial vision of loss or crisis, centering on a
question of renewal or imaginative survival; second, a despairing or
reductive answer to the question, in which the mind's power, how-
ever great, seems inadequate to overcome the obstacles both of lan-
guage and of the universe of death, of outer sense; third, a more
hopeful or at least ongoing answer, however qualified by recogni-
tions of continuing loss. Historically, this is certainly a displace-
ment of a Protestant pattern, and traces back to similar triads of
the spirit in the Psalms and the Prophets, and in Job. But however
it got there, the pattern exists, and I suggest now that it is both
more intricate and more precise than we have realized, and neces-
sarily sets the patterns of misprision also, which means of interpre-
tation as well as of revisionist or belated poetry.

Let me propose the accomplishment of an extremist in an exer-
cise: consider a Post-Enlightenment crisis-lyric of major ambitions
and rare achievement, wholly in the abstract, rather in the en-
quiring spirit of an imaginary chess game. We start then with a
strong latecomer poem. Applying the Lurianic dialectics to my
own litany of evasions, one could say that a breaking-of-the-vessels

always intervenes between every *primary* (limiting) and every *antithetical* (representing) movement that a latecomer's poem makes in relation to a precursor's text. When the latecomer initially swerves (*clinamen*) from his poetic father, he brings about a contraction or withdrawal of meaning from the father, and makes/ breaks his own false creation (fresh wandering or error-about-poetry). The anwering movement, *antithetical* to this *primary*, is the link called *tessera*, a completion that is also an opposition, or restorer of some of the degrees-of-difference between ancestral text and the new poem. This is the Lurianic pattern of *Zimzum* ⟶ *Shevirath ha-kelim* ⟶ *Tikkun*, and is enacted again (in a finer tone) in the next dialectical pair of ratios, *kenosis* (or undoing as discontinuity) and *daemonization* (the breakthrough to a personalized Counter-Sublime). Concluding the poem is an even more strenuous pattern of contraction ⟶ catastrophe ⟶ restitution, a dialectical alternation of a severer self-curtailment (*askesis*) and an answering return of lost voices and almost-abandoned meanings (*apophrades*).

The poem's opening *clinamen* is marked by dialectical images of absence and presence, images that rhetorically are conveyed by the trope of simple irony (irony as figure of speech, and not as figure of thought) and that as psychic defense assume the shape of what Freud called reaction-formation, *Reaktionsbildung*. Just as rhetorical irony or *illusio* (Quintilian's name for it) says one thing and means another, even the opposite thing, so a reaction-formation opposes itself to a repressed desire by manifesting the opposite of the desire. This is what Freud called the "primary symptom of defense," just as simple irony or *illusio* is the primary trope, the initial swerve into the error of figuration. Severe neurotic conflict frequently is manifested by rigidity or cramping in the personality, a kind of *illusio* of the spirit, such as lust transparently masking itself as forced control of behavior. But dialectical images of presence and absence, when manifested in a poem rather than a person, convey a saving atmosphere of freshness, however intense or bewildering the loss of meaning. The poem, in order to *open* in every sense, makes its initial limitation with some considerable sense of relief. It is as though the *illusio* said: "Accept absence as presence and begin by falling, for otherwise how can you *begin?*"

What follows in the poem is the antithetical completion of its first movement through the imagistic substitution of whole for part, or the transformation of *illusio* into synecdoche through seeing that somehow all presence is at least part of a mutilated whole anyway. The defensive analogues illuminate here through their contrast with one another, showing that we have moved from the psychic area of neurotic conflict in *clinamen* into the richer area of ambivalence and what Freud called "vicissitudes of instinct" (among which masochism is most prominent). Like *illusio*, reaction-formation is a contracting movement, but just as synecdoche represents macrocosm through microcosm, so the antithetical defenses of reversal-into-the-opposite and turning-aggression-against-the-self represent a lost wholeness of instinct through vicissitudes. *Reversal-into-the-opposite* is a *tessera* or ambivalent completion because it is a process in which an instinctual aim is converted into its opposite *by turning from activity to passivity*, as in the instance of the sadist being transformed into a masochist. Closely allied is the turning-aggression-against-the-self in which the threatened instinct replaces an other by the subject's own self, as though the microcosm had to suffer precisely because it represented the macrocosm. The bewilderment that always accompanies masochism is profoundly analogous to the "Where is it now?" question that so frequently ends, explicit or implicitly, the opening movement of crisis-poems.

With the middle movement we enter a very different area, imagistically and psychically. Broadly, the spirit limits itself here through repetition-compulsion, and then restitutes itself through the terrible representations that approximate hysteria, in persons rather than in poems. In *kenosis*, the poem resorts to images of reduction, frequently from fullness to emptiness. The characteristic trope here is metonymy, a change of name, or substituting the ex-

ternal aspect of a thing for the thing itself, a displacement by con-
tiguity that repeats what is displaced, but always with a lesser tone.
Here the triad of limiting defenses can be extraordinarily illumi-
nating, and takes us close to the magical affinities of poetry. Un-
doing, Freud's *Ungeschehenmachen*, is an obsessional process in
which past actions and thoughts are rendered null and void by
being repeated in a magically opposite way, a way deeply contami-
nated by what it attempts to negate. Isolation segregates thoughts
or acts so as to break their connecting links with all other thoughts
or acts, usually by breaking up temporal sequence. Regression, the
most poetically and magically active of these three obsessional de-
fenses, is a reversion to earlier phases of development, frequently
manifested through expressive modes less complex than present
ones. Where the synecdoche of *tessera* made a totality, however
illusive, the metonymy of *kenosis* breaks this up into discontinuous
fragments. We are moving towards the figure of a figure, while re-
maining in the simpler falsification that philosophers and psycholo-
gists alike term the irreality of reification. Psychologically, a *kenosis*
is not a return to origins, but is a sense that the separation from
origins is doomed to keep repeating itself. Its three constituent de-
fenses are all defenses of limitation because they all fragmentize,
preparing the ruined way for the over-restituting movement of
daemonization, the repression or hyperbole that becomes a belated
or counter-Sublime.

To write in praise of repression is only to say that *antithetical*
criticism must drive a wedge between sublimation and poetic
meaning, and so depart from Freud. The central argument of this
book, as of *The Anxiety of Influence*, is that sublimation is a *de-
fense of limitation* even as metaphor is a self-contradictory *trope of
limitation*. What the Romantics called creative Imagination is
akin, not to sublimation and metaphor, but to repression and hy-
perbole, which represent rather than limit. Repression, Freud's
Verdrängung, is a defensive process by which we try to keep in-
stinctual representations (memories and desires) unconscious. But

this attempt to keep representations unconscious actually *creates* the unconscious (though to assert this is again to depart from Freud). No deep student of poetry could agree that "the essence of repression lies simply in turning something away, and keeping it at a distance, from the conscious." Hyperbole, the trope of excess or of the over-throw, like repression finds its images in height and depth, in the Sublime and the Grotesque. To drive down into the unconscious is the same process as heaping up the unconscious, for the unconscious, like the Romantic Imagination, has *no* referential aspect. Like the Imagination, it cannot be defined because it is a Sublime trope or hyperbole, a cast of the spirit. When the poem has endured such emptying-out that its continuity threatens to be broken off, then it represses its representing force until it achieves the Sublime or falls into grotesque byways, but in either case it has produced meaning. The glory of repression, poetically speaking, is that memory and desire, driven down, have no place to go *in language* except up onto the heights of sublimity, the ego's exultation in its own operations.

With this climax of the poem's second movement, we move into the tricky limitations of *askesis*—the perspectivizing confusions of metaphor, at once the most-praised and most-failing of Western tropes. We move also into the psychic area that Freud characterized as "normality," by means of sublimation, the one "successful" defense. My suggestion here is that psychic "normality," however desirable for persons, does not work for and in poems, and that metaphor, which we might call the normal trope, drives the poem into hopeless dualistic images of inside as opposed to outside. Poems triumph by triumphing over the limitations of their own metaphors, and Post-Miltonic poems tend to know this in their patterns, by replacing metaphors by schemes of transumption, or versions of the ancient trope of metalepsis that I will expound shortly. But that will take us to our abstract poem's closing representation, its *apophrades* or attempt to make of its belatedness an earliness. More needs to be said first on the limitations of metaphor, and on the too happily dualistic defense of sublimation.

Even as metaphor condenses through resemblance, so sublimation also transfers or carries a name to an inapplicable object. In Freud's endeavor, sublimation carries the name of sexuality to thinking and to art, for Freudian *Sublimierung* is a condensation founded on the supposed resemblances between sexuality and intellectual activity, including poetry. Poetry is the outside term, and sexuality the inside one, in this unconvincing trope. No other defense is so praised by Freud and the Freudians, and no other defense is so incoherently described. Freud should have developed his own suggestion that it is aggressive impulses, rather than sexual ones, that are sublimated in philosophy and poetry, which would have brought his idea of sublimation closer to Plato and indeed also to Nietzsche. For the poem, perspectivism and its failures are crucial, since in a poem the inside/outside spectrum of images is never very satisfying. The polarities of subject and object defeat every metaphor that attempts to unify them, and it is this characteristic defeat that both defines and limits metaphor.

From Milton through the High Romantics down to the best poetry of our own moment, the limitations of metaphor are restituted by a final representation which is a metalepsis or transumption—the revisionist trope proper and the ultimate poetic resource of belatedness. It is no accident that so many important poems of the last two hundred years conclude with an imagistic movement from inside/outside polarities to early/late reversals. *Apophrades*, the Lurianic *gilgul*, is in Freudian terms a kind of paranoia, when it appears in persons rather than in poems. The Freudian defenses here are related yet antithetical to one another, being projection (which can manifest itself as jealousy) and introjection (which can manifest itself as identification). As the poetic equivalents are either proleptic representation (prophecy) or "preposterous" representation (farce, however apocalyptic) we might do well to clarify by starting with the defenses, and then passing on to the even more complex trope.

Introjection was first formulated by Ferenczi, but its coherence as a defense is largely due to Freud's linkage of it to oral incorporation. It is a fantasy transposition of otherness to the self, and as an identification seeks to defend against time and space, among other dangers. Projection seeks to expel from the self everything that the self cannot bear to acknowledge as being its own. Whereas introjection incorporates an object or an instinct so as to defend against it (thus overcoming object-relationships), projection attributes outwardly all prohibited instincts or objects to others. It should be noted that both these defenses *represent*, in that both hold forth the possibility of extending both space and time, and particularly time. More crucially, of all defenses these trope most directly against other defenses, particularly of the obsessive or repetitive-compulsive kind. This is the analogical link to the trope of metalepsis, which is a trope-reversing trope, a figure of a figure. In a metalepsis, a word is substituted metonymically for a word in a previous trope, so that a metalepsis can be called, maddeningly but accurately, a metonymy of a metonymy.

Quintilian, in defining metalepsis and in giving it the Latin name transumption, deprecated the trope and said it was good only for comedy. One might call the modern history of transumption "the trope's revenge," for from the Renaissance through Romanticism to the present day it has become the major mode of poetic allusion, and the figure without which poems would not know how to end. The prevalence of transumptive allusion is the largest single factor in fostering a tone of conscious rhetoricity in Romantic and Post-Romantic poetry. To transume means "to take across," and as a transfer of terms we can define transumption as a taking across to the poem's farther shore. Quintilian uneasily saw this as a change-of-meaning trope, since it provided a transition from one trope to another: "It is the nature of *metalepsis* to form a kind of intermediate step between the term transferred and the thing to which it is transferred, having no meaning in itself, but merely providing a transition." For no meaning in itself, say rather no presence or time in itself, for transumption can seem comic through its surrender of the living present.

Some modern rhetoricians regard metalepsis as being only an extended metaphor with a central term left out, but the Elizabethan Puttenham is closer to it when he dubs it the far-fetcher or "farrefet:"

> . . . as when we had rather fetch a word a great way off than to use one nerer hand to expresse the matter aswel and plainer. And it seemeth the deviser of this figure, had a desire to please women rather than men: for we use to say by manner of Proverbe: things farrefet and dear bought are good for Ladies: so in this manner of speech we use it, leaping over the heads of a great many words, we take one that is furdest off, to utter our matter by. . . .

The metalepsis leaps over the heads of other tropes and becomes a representation set against time, sacrificing the present to an idealized past or hoped-for future. As a figure of a figure, it ceases to be a reduction or a limitation and becomes instead a peculiar representation, either proleptic or "preposterous," in the root sense of making the later into the earlier. As a defense, this *apophrades* chooses between introjection and projection, between a kind of identification and a kind of dangerous jealousy. Either there is a spitting-out and so a distancing of the future and so a swallowing-up, an identifying with the past, by substituting late words for earlier words in an anterior trope, or else there is a distancing, a projecting of the past, and an identifying with the future, by making a substitution of early for late words. In Milton, as a later chapter in this book will show, the merging of metalepsis with allusion produces the language's most powerful instance of a poet subsuming all his precursors and making of the subsuming process much of the program and meaning of his work. Post-Miltonic developments accounted for the metaleptic reversal that dominates the imagery of the closing lines of many major Romantic and Post-Romantic poems.

In coming to the end of our map of misprision, two large questions remain unanswered. First, what is the theoretical basis for the division between ratios, tropes, defenses, and images of limitation, and those of representation? Second, how comprehensive and useful can our map be, anyway? Does not the principle of rhetorical substitution, operative in any skilled poet at will, make it unlikely that more than a handful of poems will follow our abstract model?

The first question can be answered only in the terms and context of a fuller theory of the psychoesthetics of literary representation than has yet been given us, though important suggestions have been made by Bernheimer and by Hartman. Hartman has proposed, instead of the traditional Freudian stimulus and response model, a more complex model in which an unbalanced excess of demand gives rise to a necessary defect of response on the poet's part. Relating the excess of demand to an "anxiety for language," Hartman arrives at a triple formula for the psychic function of art: limiting a demand, reinforcing a potentiality for response, or substituting either the demand or the response, one for the other. This is very close to the Lurianic dialectic that I displaced into aesthetic language in my Introduction. Reinforcing a potentiality for response is akin to representation: a poem would like to be whole, high and early, and to abound in presence, fullness, innerness. But the limitation of demand compels one group of ratios to image absence, emptiness and outsideness. I would postulate that while both the ratios of limitation and of representation substitute for one another, limitations turn away from a lost or mourned object towards either the substitute or the mourning subject, while representations turn back towards restoring the powers that desired and possessed the object. Representation points to a lack, just as limitation does, but in a way that *re-finds* what could fill the lack. Or, more simply: tropes of limitation also represent, of course, but they tend to limit the demands placed upon language by pointing to a lack both in language and the self, so that limitation really means recognition in this context. Tropes of representation also acknowledge a limit, point to a lack, but they tend to strengthen both language and the self.

The second question, as to the applicability of the map of misprision, must take an even more tentative answer. Later chapters in this book, starting with the next (on Browning's *Childe Roland*) will attempt to demonstrate the use of this model for practical criticism, for the quest of how to read a poem. A remarkable number of poems, from the *Intimations* Ode to *The Auroras of Autumn*, will be shown to follow this model of the six ratios quite closely. But variants and displacements of course abound, though generally in clearly discernible schemes of re-arrangement. One, frequent in the Age of Sensibility, tends to reverse the middle movement, with *daemonization* preceding *kenosis*. Another, characteristically American, begins the entire poem with this reversed middle movement, and then goes on to the *askesis/apophrades* pairing, before concluding with what would be the first movement of an English Romantic crisis-poem. And, necessarily, there are many poems that rebel from the model, though the rebellion is frequently equivocal. What matters is not the exact order of the ratios, but the principle of substitution, in which representations and limitations perpetually answer one another. The strength of any poet is in his skill and inventiveness at substitution, and the map of misprision is no bed of Procrustes.

6

Testing the map: Browning's *Childe Roland*

The reader, like Browning's belated quester, might wish to separate origins from aims, but the price of internalization, in poetic as in human romance, is that aims wander back towards origins. A study of misprision, as outlined in my previous chapter, allows the reader to see that interpretation of Browning's great poem is mocked by the poem itself, since Roland's monologue is his sublime and grotesque exercise of the will-to-power over the interpretation of his own text. Roland rides with us as interpreter; his every interpretation is a powerful misreading; and yet the union of those misreadings enables him to accept destruction in the triumphant realization that his ordeal, his trial by landscape, has provided us with one of the most powerful of texts that any hero-villain since Milton's Satan has given us.

The poem's opening swerve is marked rhetorically by the trope of irony, imagistically by an interplay of presence and absence, and psychologically by Roland's reaction-formation against his own destructive impulses. All this is as might be expected, but Browning's enormous skill at substitution is evident as his poem gets underway, for the strong poet shows his saving difference from himself as well as others even in his initial phrases. Roland says one thing and means another, and both the saying and the meaning seek to void a now intolerable presence. For a Post-Enlightenment poem to begin, it must know and demonstrate that nothing is in its right place.

Displacement affects at once the precursor and the poet's own earlier or idealized self, as these were a near-identity. But the precursor, like the idealized self, does not locate only in the super-ego or ego ideal. For a poet, both the youth he was and his imaginative father reside also in the poetic equivalent of the id. In Romantic quest or internalized romance, an object of desire or even a sublimated devotion to an abstract idea cannot replace the precursor-element in the id, but it does replace the ego ideal, as Freud posited. For Roland, the Dark Tower has been put in the place of the ego ideal of traditional quest, but the obsessed Childe remains haunted by precursor-forces and traces of his own former self in the id. Against these forces, his psyche has defended itself by the cramping reaction-formation of his *will-to-fail*, his perverse and negative stance that begins the poem.

Browning asks us to "see Edgar's song in *Lear*" so as to provide an epigraph to go with his poem's title, but I offer instead a sentence from Kierkegaard's *Journals* to serve as Roland's motto:

> The difference between a man who faces death for the sake of an idea and an imitator who goes in search of martyrdom is that whilst the former expresses his idea most fully in death it is the strange feeling of bitterness which comes from failure that the latter really enjoys; the former rejoices in his victory, the latter in his suffering.
>
> [March, 1836]

I think that we can test any interpretation of *Childe Roland to the Dark Tower Came* by this Kierkegaardian distinction. Is Roland finally a hero who faces death for an idea's sake, and if so, for what idea? Or is he, even at the end, what he wills to be at the start and throughout his ride to the Tower, merely an imitator who desires to enjoy the bitterness of failure? Browning is more devious than even Browning could have known, and the great, broken music of the closing stanzas, which *seems* to rejoice in victory, may be only an apotheosis of a poet suffering as poet an apocalyptic consciousness of having failed to become himself. We become great, Kierkegaard always insisted, in proportion to the greatness we fight against, whether that greatness belong to a man, an idea, a system or a poem. Does Roland, at the close, struggle against a greatness, and if so, to whom or what does it belong? How are we to read his poem?

> My first thought was, he lied in every word,
> > That hoary cripple, with malicious eye
> > Askance to watch the working of his lie
> On mine, and mouth scarce able to afford
> Suppression of the glee, that pursed and scored
> > Its edge, at one more victim gained thereby.

Roland's consciousness is grounded in the realization that *meaning has wandered already*, and in a despair at ever bringing it back. "First thought" here is not opposed to a second or later thought, which actually never enters the poem, and so "first thought" itself is an irony or the beginning of one. For Roland indeed is saying one thing while meaning another, and what he means is that the cripple inevitably speaks the truth. I take pleasure, retrospectively, having published a less advanced reading of this poem earlier (in *The Ringers in the Tower*, 1971) in now finding a critical precursor in the formidable Mrs. Sutherland Orr. That strong-minded disciple of Browning anticipated Betty Miller, George Ridenour and myself in her acute suspicions of Roland's reliability:

> So far the picture is consistent; but if we look below its surface discrepancies appear. The Tower is much nearer and more accessible than Childe Roland has thought; a sinister-looking man, of whom he asked the way, and who, as he believed, was deceiving him, has really put him on the right track; and as he describes the country through which he passes, it becomes clear that half its horrors are created by his own heated imagination. . . .

But the third stanza shows that Roland never believed the cripple was deceiving him, since in it Roland speaks of "that ominous tract which, *all agree,* hides the Dark Tower," the tract being where the cripple directed him. Still, Mrs. Orr came close to the right interpretative principle, which is to be fairly suspicious of everything Roland says, and highly suspicious of nearly everything he says he sees, at least until his final vision.

On the model of the map of misprision, *Childe Roland* is a poem in three parts: stanzas I-VIII, IX-XXIX, XXX-XXXIV. Stanzas I-VIII are the induction, during which an initial contraction or withdrawal of meaning is gradually redressed by a substitution or representation of the quest. Rhetorically, irony yields to synecdoche, psychologically a reaction-formation gives way to a turning-against-the-self, and imagistically a total sense of absence is replaced by a restituting sense of some partial significance, with a larger representation, a lost wholeness, still kept in abeyance:

> Thus, I had so long suffered in this quest,
> > Heard failure prophesied so oft, been writ
> > So many times among "The Band"—to wit,
> The knights who to the Dark Tower's search addressed
> Their steps—that just to fail as they, seemed best,
> > And all the doubt was now—should I be fit?

A desire that one be fit to fail—though this is a reversal of quest, it is yet an advance on the poem's opening, an antithetical completion of that ironic swerve from origins. Any quest is a synecdoche for the whole of desire; a quest for failure is a synecdoche for suicide. What is unique to the figurations of the first part of Browning's poem is Roland's twisted pride in his own sense of election to "The Band" of questers. This rhetorical first movement ends with stanza VIII:

> So, quiet as despair, I turned from him,
> > That hateful cripple, out of his highway
> > Into the path he pointed. All the day
> Had been a dreary one at best, and dim
> Was settling to its close, yet shot one grim
> > Red leer to see the plain catch its estray.

"Estray" is founded on *extra* + *vagare,* to wander beyond limits or out of the right way. Roland is an estray, a hyperbolic wanderer, whose dominant trait is extravagance, the Binswangerian V*erstiegenheit,* the state of having climbed to a height from which one cannot descend safely. The "grim red leer" of the sunset marks the transition to the poem's second movement (IX-XXIX), its ordeal-by-landscape.

This sequence of stanzas alternates between the psychic defense of isolation and the more Sublime defense of repression, but collapsed here into the Grotesque:

> Then came a bit of stubbed ground, once a wood,
>   Next a marsh, it would seem, and now mere earth
>   Desperate and done with; (so a fool finds mirth,
> Makes a thing and then mars it, till his mood
> Changes and off he goes!) within a rood—
>   Bog, clay and rubble, sand and stark black dearth.
>
> Now blotches rankling, coloured gay and grim,
>   Now patches where some leanness of the soil's
>   Broke into moss or substances like boils;
> Then came some palsied oak, a cleft in him
> Like a distorted mouth that splits its rim
>   Gaping at death, and dies while it recoils.

This landscape is a landscape of repetition, but in the deadliest sense, one in which all questions of genesis have yielded to mere process, to one-thing-after-another. Here, in the long middle part of Browning's poem, one is in a world of contiguities, in which resemblances, if they manifest themselves at all, must be grotesque. Roland describes his landscape like Zola describing an urban scene, yet Roland's world is wholly visionary, its "realism" a pure self-imposition. Roland's landscape is a kind of continuous metonymy, in which a single, negative aspect of every thing substitutes for the thing itself. When the dialectic of restitution seeks to operate in this middle part of the poem, it substitutes for this emptying-out-by-isolation with a hyperbolic vision of the heights; yet this is a nightmare Sublime:

For, looking up, aware I somehow grew,
  'Spite of the dusk, the plain had given place
  All round to mountains—with such name to grace
Mere ugly heights and heaps now stolen in view.
  How thus they had surprised me,—solve it, you!
  How to get from them was no clearer case.

Repression, even if unconscious, is still a purposeful process, and the reader can solve the "how" of Roland's being surprised, by an awareness of the characteristic workings of repression. Roland has forgotten (on purpose) or willed (in his depths) not to be aware of both an inward impulse (suicidal self-punishment) and an outer event (the failure of his precursors in "The Band"), both of which tempt him towards yielding to instinctual demands that his ego-ideal finds objectionable. These demands would merge him into his landscape of dearth, and can be termed nihilistic, in the full and uncanny sense best defined by Nietzsche. Roland too would rather have the void as purpose than be void of purpose, yet his wayward impulses court every evidence of purposelessness. For Roland, despite his overt allegiance to his Band of precursors, is a revisionist strong poet, and so a hero-villian, even of and in his own poem. His misprision or mis-taking of his inherited quest-pattern culminates in stanza XXIX, which ends the second movement of the poem:

Yet half I seemed to recognize some trick
  Of mischief happened to me, God knows when—
  In a bad dream perhaps. Here ended, then,
Progress this way. When, in the very nick
Of giving up, one time more, came a click
  As when a trap shuts—you're inside the den!

In the nick or crucial moment of giving up, which would be the prolongation of a wholly negative repetition, Roland is suddenly startled into a climactic recognition, which is that he is trapped, yet paradoxically this entrapment alone makes possible a fulfillment of his quest. Just here, before the poem proceeds to its final movement, the problem of interpretation is most difficult. The meaning of *Childe Roland to the Dark Tower Came* is most problematic in its last five stanzas, which alternate between an *askesis* of defeated metaphor and a magnificent, perhaps triumphant metaleptic return of earlier powers.

What are we to make of Roland's perspectivism, his metaphoric juxtapositions between inside and outside?

> Burningly it came on me all at once,
>   This was the place! those two hills on the right,
>   Crouched like two bulls locked horn in horn in fight;
> While to the left, a tall scalped mountain . . . Dunce,
> Dotard, a-dozing at the very nonce,
>   After a life spent training for the sight!

Metaphors for art as an activity tend to center upon a particular place, where a heightened sense of presence can manifest itself. This is a place, as Hartman says, both of heightened demand and of an intensified consciousness that attempts to meet such demand by an increased power of representation. Browning's Roland, exultantly proclaiming: "This was the place!" brings together most of the crucial variants of the metaphor for art as an activity. Roland confronts at once a staged scene, a court of judgment (his failed precursors in "The Band"), and, most heroically, an initiation, a purgatorial induction parallel to that of Keats in *The Fall of Hyperion* or Shelley in *The Triumph of Life*. Part of the resonance, the strong sense of inevitability, in the next stanza, is due to Browning's perfect choice of the Dark Tower as the ultimate metaphor for art's Scene of Instruction:

> What in the midst lay but the Tower itself?
>   The round squat turret, blind as the fool's heart,
>   Built of brown stone, without a counterpart
> In the whole world. The tempest's mocking elf
> Points to the shipman thus the unseen shelf
>   He strikes on, only when the timbers start.

Shall we, tentatively, call both the Dark Tower and the mocking elf the Oedipal necessities of self-betrayal in the practice of art? Or, more narrowly, the Tower and the elf are metaphors for misprision, for the over-determined and inescapable meanings that belated creators impose upon poetic tradition. The Tower stands for the blindness of the influence-process, which is the same as the reading-process. Fresh creation is a catastrophe, or a substitution, a making-breaking that is performed in blindness. The elf mocks by pointing to the unseen hazard "only when the timbers start," which is after the new poem has been begotten by blindness upon blindness. Roland is giving us a parable of his relation to his brother-knights, which becomes a parable of Browning's relation to the poets who quested for the Dark Tower before him.

The Tower *is* Dark because it stands for the possibilities and therefore also the limitations of metaphor as such, which means for the blindness of all inside/outside perspectivisms. The paradox of perspectivism, as outlined in the previous chapter, is that it depends wholly on the subject/object dualism, while attempting to be a way of seeing more clearly. It is not accidental that the greatest perspectivist in poetry is Milton's Satan, for the effect of an absolute perspectivism is to bring about a subjective dissolving of all knowledge, and so an ebbing away of the distinction between factual truth and falsity. As much as the tautologies of the solipsist, the perspectivism of Satan (or of Roland) is necessarily self-contradictory. The Dark Tower lay in the midst, but for Roland there can be no "midst"; and his inability to see the Tower as such, after a lifetime training for the sight, is enormously instructive.

But Browning, and Roland, do not end with limiting and so with failed metaphor:

> Not see? because of night perhaps?—why, day
>   Came back again for that! before it left,
>   The dying sunset kindled through a cleft:
> The hills, like giants at a hunting, lay,
> Chin upon hand, to see the game at bay,—
>   "Now stab and end the creature—to the heft!"

Not hear? when noise was everywhere! it tolled
    Increasing like a bell. Names in my ears
    Of all the lost adventurers my peers,—
How such a one was strong, and such was bold,
And such was fortunate, yet each of old
    Lost, lost! one moment knelled the woe of years.

These stanzas, together with the last one, which follows them, constitute a transumptive scheme or figure of a figure, which undoes the figurative assertions of Roland throughout the entire poem before them. Roland is belated, the last of the Band, and yet of his belatedness he now makes (and breaks) an earliness, at the apparent expense of his life. The act of representation here is both proleptic, foretelling a future that lies just beyond the span of the poem, and "preposterous," inverting the quest-pattern by revealing the past failures as being something other than failures. What are we to interpret Roland's "day came back again for that!" as meaning? Realistically, it may tell us that Roland's time-sense in the long middle part of the poem is a delusion, for "the dying sunset kindled" may be identical with the "red leer" of the sun at the end of stanza VIII. Whether that is so, or whether the last kindling of sunset is a kind of lapse in nature, either way Roland is troping upon and so undoing an earlier trope. He thus calls attention to the rhetoricity of his closing statement by raising both his own word-consciousness and that of his reader, in a manner rather akin to Nietzsche's in *Zarathustra*. His rhetorical questions "Not see?" and "Not hear?" become hyperboles of hyperboles, and place the poem's previously grotesque sublimities in considerable doubt. What he *sees* is the place of trial, scene of his true ordeal, which is not to be by landscape, but by the return of his precursors. What he *hears* are the celebrated names of the precursors and the causes for the celebration, strength and loss tolling together in one increasing dirge. What remains is vision proper, as the once-ruined quester is transformed into a seer. Where earlier we distrusted everything Roland told us he saw, now we see feelingly all that he tells:

> There they stood, ranged along the hill-sides, met
>   To view the last of me, a living frame
>   For one more picture! in a sheet of flame
> I saw them and I knew them all. And yet
> Dauntless the slug-horn to my lips I set,
>   And blew. *"Childe Roland to the Dark Tower came."*

The perspectivism of the Dark Tower metaphor has been over-come by that final line, where the Childe presents himself as the limner of his own night-piece, the poet rather than the subject of his poem. The precursor-questers meet to view the last of Roland, as an outside to his inside, but he has attained what Yeats was to call the Condition of Fire, and in that flame he views the last of them, and unlike them he both sees and *knows* what he sees. Because he has attained knowledge and is transformed, they no longer know him. Undefeated by his total knowledge, he abandons the world of romance and enters prophecy, by setting the slug-horn of the tragic, suicidal, too-early Romantic poet Chatterton to his lips. What he blows is his poem, as we have to read it, the trumpet of a prophecy because of its transumptive relation to Romantic prophecy.

So far we have read *Childe Roland* as a revisionary text, on the model of our map of misprision. But on the larger model of our Scene of Instruction, as described in Chapter 3, this is only the first level of interpretation (the rhetorical, psychological and imagistic one) in the hierarchy of how to read a poem. We need to ask next: What is the interpretation of tradition, and in particular of the central precursor or precursors, that this poem's revisionary ratios give us? Moving up our ladder of interpretation, we then will contrast the Word brought forward by the later poet with the rival Word of his father. Next we will climb to a contrast of rival inspirations or muses, and beyond that to a consideration of the Covenant-love between the two poets, or more simply, the pact explicit or implicit that the latecomer makes with the earlier poet. Finally, we will consider the Election-love between the poets, that is to say, why the later poet felt himself Chosen or found by the earlier poet, and what difference that made in his sense of vocation.

It is important to notice that so far I have excluded from this discussion virtually all consideration of the poetic tradition that formed Browning, as well as an account of Browning's relation to a specific precursor, and also what generally would be termed the "sources" of *Childe Roland to the Dark Tower Came*. My motive is to distinguish once for all what I call "poetic influence" from traditional "source study." Antithetical criticism as a practical discipline of reading begins with an analysis of misprision or revisionism, through a description of revisionary ratios, conducted through examination of tropes, imagery or psychological defenses, depending upon the preferences of an individual reader. An application of literary history, though greatly desirable, is not strictly necessary for the study of misprision. But as soon as one attempts a deeper criticism, and asks what is the interpretation that a poem offers, one is involved with the precursor text or texts as well as with the belated poem itself.

Shelley is the Hidden God of the universe created by *Childe Roland to the Dark Tower Came*. His is the presence that the poem labors to void, and his is the force that rouses the poem's force. Out of that struggle between forces rises the form of Browning's poem, which is effectively the *difference* between the rival strengths of poetic father and poetic son. I would agree with Paul de Man that all strong poems contain an authentically self-negating element, a genuinely epistemological moment, but always I would insist that this moment comes in *their relationship to a prior poem*, a relationship that remains inescapably subject-to-subject centered. In *Childe Roland*, this moment is reserved for the end, for the final stanza. There Roland negates the larger part of his poem, a negation that strengthens rather than weakens the poem, because there Roland suffers a unique act of knowledge, an act that clarifies both his personal past and tradition, though at the expense of both presence and the present. By "presence" I mean both Roland's self-presence, and also the virtual existence of any opposing force in the poem other than Roland's internalization of the precursors.

Let me offer an explicit, indeed a reductive and therefore simpli-
fied total interpretation of the poem, firmly based on the model of
misprision I have been tracing. There is no ogre at or in the Dark
Tower for Roland to confront; the Tower is windowless and unin-
habited, as blind as Roland's own fool's heart. "Fool" as a word
goes back to the Latin *follis* for "bellows," and so a fool originally
was a windbag. The root *bhel* means to blow or swell, which gives
a triumphant twist to Roland's final act of blowing his slug-horn.
In the *Song of Roland* this act is a signal to Roland's friends and is
at the expense of almost the last breath of the mortally wounded
hero. But Childe Roland's friends are disgraced and dead, and only
the Childe's heart has been wounded, by the blind foolishness of
questing for failure. Yet we feel, as readers, that death or at least
mortal combat must be at hand as the poem ends. If Roland is
alone at the end, as he is throughout the poem, then who is the
antagonist? Certainly not "The Band" of brothers and precursors,
for they stand ranged in vision, at the close. They may be a court
in judgment, but they are there to see and to be seen, not to act.

There is only Roland himself to serve both as hero and as villain,
only Roland to sound the trumpet as warning against Roland. The
Childe stands in judgment against his own antithetical quest and,
however lovingly, against his antithetical precursors as well. His
blast on the slug-horn is an interpretation of his precursors' quest,
which is to say that the poem becomes Browning's interpretation
of a poem like Shelley's *Ode to the West Wind*, and perhaps of
all Shelley's poetry. Roland sees himself at last as what he is, the
solitary poet-quester, the *penseroso* so dangerously internalized as
to have become anti-natural or antithetical, a counter-placing fig-
ure who stands against all the continuities that make life possible
for the natural man. Roland is the culmination, akin to Tennyson's
Ulysses, of the development undergone by his immediate ances-
tors: Wordsworth's Solitary in *The Excursion*, Byron's Childe
Harold, Shelley's poet-wanderer in *Alastor* and in *Prince Athanase*.
One can recall the lines by Shelley in his *Athanase* fragment that
perpetually haunted Yeats:

His soul had wedded Wisdom, and her dower
Is love and justice, clothed in which he sate
Apart from men, as in a lonely tower,

Pitying the tumult of their dark estate.

Roland's tower is closer to the less idealized tower of Shelley's *Julian and Maddalo*:

I looked, and saw between us and the sun
A building on an island; such a one
As age to age might add, for uses vile,
A windowless, deformed and dreary pile;
And on the top an open tower, where hung
A bell, which in the radiance swayed and swung;
We could just hear its hoarse and iron tongue:
The broad sun sunk behind it, and it tolled
In strong and black relief.

We can juxtapose to this a passage from Browning's *Essay on Shelley*, where Browning portrays himself as he would have been, a dramatic or "objective" poet rather than a Shelleyan "subjective" poet like Roland:

Did the personality of such an one stand like an open watch-tower in the midst of the territory it is erected to gaze on . . . ? Or did some sunken and darkened chamber of imagery witness . . . how rare and precious were the outlooks through here and there an embrasure upon a world beyond . . . ?

Roland has come, not to an open watch-tower, whether of Athanase's or Browning's "objective" poet, but to the madhouse of *Julian and Maddalo*. His solipsism, sustained to the ultimate "realism" of his ordeal-by-landscape, would be total and therefore a madness if it were not for his final vision of his precursors, a vision that saves his sense of otherness and so still gives him purposiveness, thus bestowing meaning upon his last act. Yet the phantasmagoria of his final quest was due to his horror of the past, his dread of failing as his precursors failed, a dread that nevertheless become the sympathetic antipathy (as Kierkegaard called his concept of Dread) that motivated his quest. Roland has triumphed by failing precisely as his precursors failed, and by recognizing and so *knowing* that their "failure" was a triumph also. Each one in turn found himself alone at the Dark Tower, facing himself as opponent at the Scene of Instruction, measuring himself always against the composite form of the forerunners. The Dark Tower is the self-negating element in the activity of art, and Roland is the poetic consciousness at its most dangerous to itself and to all others, burning through nature and so through everything in the self that is not the imagination.

As misprision, *Childe Roland to the Dark Tower Came* means the interplay of tropes, defenses, images that we have been studying. As *lidrosh*, interpretation, it means a de-idealizing critique of Shelley, but a wholly loving critique, one that exposes not the generous power of Shelley's trumpet of a prophecy, but something more of the experiential cost than the remorselessly noble Shelley would deign to acknowledge. As a Word of Browning's own brought forward, *Childe Roland* contrasts with Shelley's less psychologically revealing word, for Browning is a congeries of persons, and Shelley much more of a single being. Where the inspiration of Shelley is Orphic, Browning's is more unconditioned and absolute, because closer both to solipsism and to madness. The covenant between Shelley and Browning calls for a refusal to compromise with anything not in itself solitary and imaginative, and this covenant Browning has broken, with a consequent guilt present throughout Roland's monologue. But the Election-love burns on fiercely in Browning's Condition of Fire, as it will in Yeats's, for the sense of vocation in Roland as in Browning is renewed perpetually by Shelley's uncompromising and so both inspiring and chiding example. A more total reading of *Childe Roland* than I have space for here would mount up through all these contrasts.

But something of the conclusion can be surmised here, however tentatively. Roland's equivocal triumph is an instance of Kierkegaardian "repetition" rather than of Platonic "recollection" or Hegelian "mediation," if only because the Romantic trope-upon-a-trope or transumption leads to a projective or introjective stance of which Kierkegaard is the conscious anti-Platonic and anti-Hegelian theorist. Precisely what Roland refuses is the Golgotha of Absolute Spirit that Hegel proclaims at the very close of his *Phenomenology*:

> . . . Knowledge is aware not only of itself, but also of the negative of itself, or its limit. Knowing its limit means knowing how to sacrifice itself. This sacrifice is . . . self-abandonment. . . . Here it has to begin all over again at its immediacy, as freshly as before, and thence rise once more to the measure of its stature, as if, for it, all that preceded were lost, and as if it had learned nothing from the experience of the spirits that preceded. But re-collection has conserved that experience, and is the inner being, and, in fact, the higher form of the substance. While, then, this phase of Spirit begins all over again its formative development, apparently starting solely from itself, yet at the same time it commences at a higher level. The realm of spirits developed in this way, and assuming definite shape in existence, constitutes a succession, where one detaches and sets loose the other, and each takes over from its predecessor the empire of the spiritual world. . . .

Against this high idealism of what is essentially the influence-process, we can set one of Kierkegaard's central insights:

> . . . It requires youth to hope, and youth to recollect, but it requires courage to will repetition. . . . For hope is an alluring fruit which does not satisfy, recollection is a miserable pittance which does not satisfy, but repetition is the daily bread which satisfies with benediction. When one has circumnavigated existence, it will appear whether one has courage to understand that life is a repetition, and to delight in that very fact. . . . Repetition is reality, and it is the seriousness of life. . . .

From Hegel we can move to Mallarmé's *Igitur*, and an illuminating observation by Paul de Man, even as from Kierkegaard we can go back to *Childe Roland* and the critical mode I endeavor to develop. Meditating on *Igitur*, de Man remarks that in Baudelaire and in Mallarmé (under Baudelaire's influence) "ennui" is no longer a personal feeling but comes from the burden of the past. A consciousness comes to know itself as negative and finite. It sees that others know themselves also in this way, and so it transcends the negative and finite present by seeing the universal nature of what it itself is becoming. So de Man says of Mallarmé's view, comparing it to Hegel's, that "we develop by dominating our natural anxiety and alienation and by transforming it in the awareness and the knowledge of otherness."

The difference between Hegel and Kierkegaard is also a difference between Mallarmé and Browning, as it happens, and critically a difference between a deconstructive and an antithetical view of practical criticism. Kierkegaard's "repetition" is closer than its Hegelian rival (or the Nietzschean-Heideggerian descendant) to the mutually exploitative relationships between strong poets, a mutuality that affects the dead nearly as much as the living. Insofar as a poet authentically is and remains a poet, he must exclude and negate other poets. Yet he must begin by including and affirming a precursor poet or poets, for there is no other way to become a poet. We can say then that a poet is *known as* a poet only by a wholly contradictory including/excluding, negating/affirming which by the agency of psychic defenses manifests as an introjecting/ projecting. "Repetition," better even than Nietzsche's Eternal Return of the Same, is what rhetorically manifests itself through the scheme of transumption, where the surrender of the present compensates for the contradictory movements of the psyche.

Roland is not mediated by his precursors; they do not detach him from history so as to free him in the spirit. The Childe's last act of dauntless courage is to will repetition, to accept his place in the company of the ruined. Roland tells us ımplicitly that the present is not so much negative and finite as it is willed, though this willing is never the work of an individual consciousness acting by itself. It is caught up in a subject-to-subject dialectic, in which the present moment is sacrificed, not to the energies of art, but to the near-solipsist's tragic victory over himself. Roland's negative moment is neither that of renunciation nor that of the loss of self in death or error. It is the negativity that is self-knowledge yielding its power to a doomed love of others, in the recognition that those others, like Shelley, had more grandly surrendered knowledge and its powers to love, however illusory. Or, most simply, Childe Roland dies, if he dies, in the magnificence of a belatedness that can accept itself as such. He ends in strength, because his vision has ceased to break and deform the world, and has begun to turn its dangerous strength upon its own defenses. Roland is the modern poet-as-hero, and his sustained courage to weather his own phantasmagoria and emerge into fire is a presage of the continued survival of strong poetry.

Part III
USING THE MAP

7

Milton and his precursors

No poet compares to Milton in his intensity of self-consciousness as an artist and in his ability to overcome all negative consequences of such concern. Milton's highly deliberate and knowingly ambitious program necessarily involved him in direct competition with Homer, Virgil, Lucretius, Ovid, Dante and Tasso, among other major precursors. More anxiously, it brought him very close to Spenser, whose actual influence on *Paradise Lost* is deeper, subtler and more extensive than scholarship so far has recognized. Most anxiously, the ultimate ambitions of *Paradise Lost* gave Milton the problem of expanding Scripture without distorting the Word of God.

A reader, thinking of Milton's style, is very likely to recognize that style's most distinctive characteristic as being the density of its allusiveness. Perhaps only Gray compares to Milton in this regard, and Gray is only a footnote, though an important and valuable one, to the Miltonic splendor. Milton's allusiveness has a distinct design, which is to enhance both the quality and the extent of his inventiveness. His handling of allusion is his highly individual and original defense against poetic tradition, his revisionary stance in writing what is in effect a tertiary epic, following after Homer in primary epic and Virgil, Ovid and Dante in secondary epic. Most vitally, Miltonic allusion is the crucial revisionary ratio by which *Paradise Lost* distances itself from its most dangerous precursor,

The Faerie Queene, for Spenser had achieved a national romance, of epic greatness, in the vernacular, and in the service of moral and theological beliefs not far from Milton's own.

The map of misprision charted in Chapter 5 moved between the poles of *illusio*—irony as a figure of speech, or the reaction-formation I have termed *clinamen*—and allusion, particularly as the scheme of transumption or metaleptic reversal that I have named *apophrades* and analogized to the defenses of introjection and projection. As the common root of their names indicates, *illusio* and allusion are curiously related, both being a kind of mockery, rather in the sense intended by the title of Geoffrey Hill's poem on Campanella, that "Men are a mockery of Angels." The history of "allusion" as an English word goes from an initial meaning of "illusion" on to an early Renaissance use as meaning a pun, or word-play in general. But by the time of Bacon it meant any symbolic likening, whether in allegory, parable or metaphor, as when in *The Advancement of Learning* poetry is divided into "narrative, representative, and allusive." A fourth meaning, which is still the correct modern one, follows rapidly by the very early seventeenth century, and involves any implied, indirect or hidden reference. The fifth meaning, still incorrect but bound to establish itself, now equates allusion with direct, overt reference. Since the root meaning is "to play with, mock, jest at," allusion is uneasily allied to words like "ludicrous" and "elusion," as we will remember later.

Thomas McFarland, formidably defending Coleridge against endlessly repetitive charges of plagiarism, has suggested that "plagiarism" ought to be added as a seventh revisionary ratio. Allusion is a comprehensive enough ratio to contain "plagiarism" also under the heading of *apophrades*, which the Lurianic Kabbalists called *gilgul*, as I explained in the Introduction. Allusion as covert reference became in Milton's control the most powerful and successful figuration that any strong poet has ever employed against his strong precursors.

Milton, who would not sunder spirit from matter, would not let himself be a receiver, object to a subject's influencings. His stance against dualism and influence alike is related to his exaltation of unfallen *pleasure*, his appeal not so much to his reader's senses as to his reader's yearning for the expanded senses of Eden. Precisely here is the center of Milton's own influence upon the Romantics, and here also is why he surpassed them in greatness, since what he could do for himself was the cause of their becoming unable to do the same for themselves. His achievement became at once their starting point, their inspiration, yet also their goad, their torment.

Yet he too had his starting point: Spenser. Spenser was "the soothest shepherd that e'er piped on plains," "sage and serious." "Milton has acknowledged to me, that Spenser was his original," Dryden testified, but the paternity required no acknowledgment. A darker acknowledgment can be read in Milton's astonishing mistake about Spenser in *Areopagitica*, written more than twenty years before *Paradise Lost* was completed:

> . . . It was from out the rind of one apple tasted, that the knowledge of good and evil, as two twins cleaving together, leaped forth into the world. And perhaps this is that doom which Adam fell into of knowing good and evil, that is to say of knowing good by evil. As therefore the state of man is, what wisdom can there be to choose, what continence to forbear, without the knowledge of evil? He that can apprehend and consider vice with all her baits and seeming pleasures, and yet abstain, and yet distinguish, and yet prefer that which is truly better, he is the true warfaring Christian. I cannot praise a fugitive and cloistered virtue, unexercised and unbreathed, that never sallies out and sees her adversary, but slinks out of the race, where that immortal garland is to be run for, not without dust and heat. Assuredly we bring not innocence into the world, we bring impurity much rather; that which purifies us is trial, and trial is by what is contrary. That virtue therefore which is but a youngling in the contemplation of evil, and knows not the utmost that vice promises to her followers, and rejects it, is but a blank virtue, not a pure; her whiteness is but an excremental whiteness; which was the reason why our sage and serious poet Spenser, whom I dare be known to think

a better teacher than Scotus or Aquinas, describing true temper-
ance under the person of Guyon, brings him in with his palmer
through the cave of Mammon, and the bower of earthly bliss,
that he might see and know, and yet abstain. . . .

Spenser's cave of Mammon is Milton's Hell; far more than the
descents to the underworld of Homer and Virgil, more even than
Dante's vision, the prefigurement of Books I and II of *Paradise
Lost* reverberates in Book II of *The Faerie Queene*. Against Ac-
rasia's bower, Guyon enjoys the moral guidance of his unfaltering
Palmer, but necessarily in Mammon's cave Guyon has to be wholly
on his own, even as Adam and Eve must withstand temptation in
the absence of the affable Raphael. Guyon stands, though at some
cost; Adam and Eve fall, but both the endurance and the failure
are independent. Milton's is no ordinary error, no mere lapse in
memory, but is itself a powerful misinterpretation of Spenser, and
a strong defense against him. For Guyon is not so much Adam's
precursor as he is Milton's own, the giant model imitated by the
Abdiel of *Paradise Lost*. Milton re-writes Spenser so as to *increase
the distance* between his poetic father and himself. St. Augustine
identified memory with the father, and we may surmise that a
lapse in a memory as preternatural as Milton's is a movement
against the father.

Milton's full relation to Spenser is too complex and hidden for
any rapid description or analysis to suffice, even for my limited pur-
poses in this book. Here I will venture that Milton's transumptive
stance in regard to all his precursors, including Spenser, is founded
on Spenser's resourceful and bewildering (even Joycean) way of
subsuming his precursors, particularly Virgil, through his labyrin-
thine syncretism. Spenserian allusiveness has been described by An-
gus Fletcher as collage: "Collage is parody drawing attention to the
materials of art and life." Fletcher follows Harry Berger's descrip-
tion of the technique of *conspicuous allusion* in Spenser: "the de-
piction of stock literary motifs, characters, and genres in a manner
which emphasizes their conventionality, displaying at once their

debt to and their existence in a conventional climate—Classical, medieval, romance, etc.—which is archaic when seen from Spenser's retrospective viewpoint." This allusive collage or conspicuousness is readily assimilated to Spenser's peculiarly metamorphic elegiacism, which becomes the particular legacy of Spenser to all his poetic descendants, from Drayton and Milton down to Yeats and Stevens. For Spenser began that internalization of quest-romance that is or became what we call Romanticism. It is the Colin Clout of Spenser's Book VI who is the father of Milton's *Il Penseroso*, and from Milton's visionary stem the later Spenserian transformations of Wordsworth's Solitary, and all of the Solitary's children in the wanderers of Keats, Shelley, Browning, Tennyson and Yeats until the parodistic climax in Stevens' comedian Crispin. Fletcher, in his study of Spenser, *The Prophetic Moment*, charts this genealogy of introspection, stressing the intervention of Shakespeare between Spenser and Milton, since from Shakespeare Milton learned to contain the Spenserian elegiacism or "prophetic strain" within what Fletcher calls "transcendental forms." In his study of *Comus* as such a form, *The Transcendental Masque*, Fletcher emphasizes the "enclosed vastness" in which Milton, like Shakespeare, allows reverberations of the Spenserian resonance, a poetic diction richly dependent on allusive echoings of precursors. *Comus* abounds in *apophrades*, the return of many poets dead and gone, with Spenser and Shakespeare especially prominent among them. Following Berger and Fletcher, I would call the allusiveness of *Comus* still "conspicuous" and so still Spenserian, still part of the principle of echo. But, with *Paradise Lost*, Miltonic allusion is transformed into a mode of transumption, and poetic tradition is radically altered in consequence.

Fletcher, the most daemonic and inventive of modern allegorists, is again the right guide into the mysteries of *transumptive allusion*, through one of the brilliant footnotes in his early book, *Allegory: The Theory of a Symbolic Mode* (p. 241, n. 33). Studying what he calls "difficult ornament" and the transition to modern allegory,

Fletcher meditates on Johnson's ambivalence towards Milton's style. In his *Life of Milton*, Johnson observes that "the heat of Milton's mind might be said to sublimate his learning." Hazlitt, a less ambivalent admirer of Milton, asserted that Milton's learning had the effect of intuition. Johnson, though so much more grudging, actually renders the greater homage, for Johnson's own immense hunger of imagination was overmatched by Milton's, as he recognized:

> Whatever be his subject, he never fails to fill the imagination. But his images and descriptions of the scenes or operations of Nature do not seem to be always copied from original form, nor to have the freshness, raciness, and energy of immediate observation. He saw Nature, as Dryden expresses it, *through the spectacles of books*; and on most occasions calls learning to his assistance. . . .
> . . . But he does not confine himself within the limits of rigorous comparison: his great excellence is amplitude, and he expands the adventitious image beyond the dimensions which the occasion required. Thus, comparing the shield of Satan to the orb of the Moon, he crowds the imagination with the discovery of the telescope, and all the wonders which the telescope discovers.

This Johnsonian emphasis upon allusion in Milton inspires Fletcher to compare Miltonic allusion to the trope of transumption or metalepsis, Puttenham's "far-fetcher":

> Johnson stresses allusion in Milton: "the spectacles of books" are a means of sublimity, since at every point the reader is led from one scene to an allusive second scene, to a third, and so on. Johnson's Milton has, we might say, a "transumptive" style. . . .

Here is the passage that moved Johnson's observation, *Paradise Lost*, Book I, 283-313. Beelzebub has urged Satan to address his fallen legions, who still lie "astounded and amazed" on the lake of fire:

He scarce had ceas't when the superior Fiend
Was moving toward the shore; his ponderous shield
Ethereal temper, massy, large and round,
Behind him cast; the broad circumference
Hung on his shoulders like the Moon, whose Orb
Through Optic Glass the *Tuscan* Artist views
At Ev'ning from the top of *Fesole*,
Or in*Valdarno*, to descry new Lands,
Rivers or Mountains in her spotty Globe.
His Spear, to equal which the tallest Pine
Hewn on *Norwegian* hills, to be the Mast
Of some great Ammiral, were but a wand,
He walkt with to support uneasy steps
Over the burning Marl, not like those steps
On Heaven's Azure, and the torrid Clime
Smote on him sore besides, vaulted with Fire;
Nathless he so endur'd, till on the Beach
Of that inflamed Sea, he stood and call'd
His Legions, Angel Forms, who lay intrans't
Thick as Autumnal Leaves that strow the Brooks
In *Vallombrosa*, where th'*Etrurian* shades
High overarch't imbow'r; or scatter'd sedge
Afloat, when with fierce Winds *Orion* arm'd
Hath vext the Red-Sea Coast, whose waves o'erthrew
Busiris and his *Memphian* Chivalry,
While with perfidious hatred they pursu'd
The Sojourners of *Goshen*, who beheld
From the safe shore thir floating Carcasses
And broken Chariot Wheels, so thick bestrown
Abject and lost lay these, covering the Flood,
Under amazement of thir hideous change.

The transumption of the precursors here is managed by the juxtaposition between the far-fetching of Homer, Virgil, Ovid, Dante, Tasso, Spenser, the Bible and the single near-contemporary reference to Galileo, "the Tuscan artist," and his telescope. Milton's aim is to make his own belatedness into an earliness, and his tradition's priority over him into a lateness. The critical question to be asked of this passage is: why is Johnson's "adventitious image," Galileo and the telescope, present at all? Johnson, despite his judgment that the image is extrinsic, implies the right answer: because the expansion of this apparently extrinsic image crowds the reader's imagination, by giving Milton the true priority of *interpretation*, the powerful reading that insists upon its own uniqueness and its own accuracy. Troping upon his forerunners' tropes, Milton compels us to read as he reads, and to accept his stance and vision as our origin, his time as true time. His allusiveness introjects the past, and projects the future, but at the paradoxical cost of the present, which is not voided but is yielded up to an experiential darkness, as we will see, to a mingling of wonder (discovery) and woe (the fallen Church's imprisonment of the discoverer). As Frank Kermode remarks, *Paradise Lost* is a wholly contemporary poem, yet surely its sense of the present is necessarily more of loss than of delight.

Milton's giant simile comparing Satan's shield to the moon alludes to the shield of Achilles in the *Iliad*, XIX, 373-80:

> . . . and caught up the great shield, huge and heavy
> next, and from it the light glimmered far, as from the moon.
> And as when from across water a light shines to mariners
> from a blazing fire, when the fire is burning high in the mountains
> in a desolate standing, as the mariners are carried unwilling
> by storm winds over the fish-swarming sea, far away from their
>   loved ones;
> so the light from the fair elaborate shield of Achilleus
> shot into the high air.
>
> > [Lattimore version]

Milton is glancing also at the shield of Radigund in *The Faerie Queene*, V, v, 3:

> And on her shoulder hung her shield, bedeckt
> Upon the bosse with stones, that shined wide,
> As the faire Moone in her most full aspect,
> That to the Moone it mote be like in each respect.

Radigund, Princess of the Amazons, is dominated by pride and anger, like Achilles. Satan, excelling both in his bad eminence, is seen accurately through the optic glass of the British artist's transumptive vision, even as Galileo sees what no one before him has seen on the moon's surface. Galileo, when visited by Milton (as he tells us in *Areopagitica*), was working while under house arrest by the Inquisition, a condition not wholly unlike Milton's own in the early days of the Restoration. Homer and Spenser emphasize the moonlike brightness and shining of the shields of Achilles and Radigund; Milton emphasizes size, shape, weight as the common feature of Satan's shield and the moon, for Milton's post-Galilean moon is more of a world and less of a light. Milton and Galileo are *late*, yet they see more, and more significantly, than Homer and Spenser, who were *early*. Milton gives his readers the light, yet also the true dimensions and features of reality, even though Milton, like the Tuscan artist, must work on while compassed around by experiential darkness, in a world of woe.

Milton will not stop with his true vision of Satan's shield, but transumes his precursors also in regard to Satan's spear, and to the fallen-leaves aspect of the Satanic host. Satan's spear evokes passages of Homer, Virgil, Ovid, Tasso and Spenser, allusions transumed by the contemporary reference to a flagship ("ammiral") with its mast made of Norwegian fir. The central allusion is probably to Ovid's vision of the Golden Age (Golding's version, I, 109-16):

> The loftie Pyntree was not hewen from mountaines where it stood,
> In seeking straunge and forren landes to rove upon the flood.
> Men knew none other countries yet, than where themselves did
>   keepe:
> There was no towne enclosed yet, with walles and ditches deepe.
> No horne nor trumpet was in use, no sword nor helmet worne.
> The worlde was suche, that souldiers helpe might easly be
>   forborne.
> The fertile earth as yet was free, untoucht of spade or plough,
> And yet it yeelded of it selfe of every things inough.

Ovid's emblem of the passage from Golden Age to Iron Age is reduced to "but a wand," for Satan will more truly cause the fall from Golden to Iron. As earlier Satan subsumed Achilles and Radigund, now he contains and metaleptically reverses the Polyphemus of Homer and of Virgil, the Tancredi and Argantes of Tasso, and the proud giant Orgoglio of Spenser:

> a club, or staff, lay there along the fold—
> an olive tree, felled green and left to season
> for Kyklops' hand. And it was like a mast
> a lugger of twenty oars, broad in the beam—
> a deep-sea-going craft—might carry:
> so long, so big around, it seemed.
>
> > [*Odyssey*, IX, 322-27, Fitzgerald version]

> . . . we saw
> upon a peak the shepherd Polyphemus;
> he lugged his mammoth hulk among the flocks,
> searching along familiar shores—an awful
> misshapen monster, huge, his eyelight lost.
> His steps are steadied by the lopped-off pine
> he grips. . . .
>
> > [*Aeneid*, III, 660-66; Mandelbaum version, 849-55]

> These sons of Mavors bore, instead of spears,
>   Two knotty masts, which none but they could lift;
> Each foaming steed so fast his master bears,
>   That never beast, bird, shaft, flew half so swift:
> Such was their fury, as when Boreas tears
>   The shatter'd crags from Taurus' northern clift:
> Upon their helms their lances long they brake,
> And up to heav'n flew splinters, sparks, and smoke.
>
> > [*Jerusalem Delivered*, VI, 40; Fairfax version]

> So growen great through arrogant delight
>   Of th'high descent, whereof he was yborne,
>   And through presumption of his matchlesse might,
>   All other powres and knighthood he did scorne.
>   Such now he marcheth to this man forlorne,
>   And left to losse: his stalking steps are stayde
>   Upon a snaggy Oke, which he had torne

Out of his mothers bowelles, and it made
His mortall mace, wherewith his foemen he dismayde.
[*Faerie Queene*, I, vii, x]

The Wild Men, Polyphemus the Cyclops and the crudely proud
Orgoglio, as well as the Catholic and Circassian champions, Tan-
credi and Argantes, all become late and lesser versions of Milton's
earlier and greater Satan. The tree and the mast become inter-
changeable with the club, and all three become emblematic of the
brutality of Satan as the Antichrist, the fallen son of God who
walks in the darkness of his vainglory and perverts nature to the
ends of war-by-sea and war-by-land, Job's Leviathan and Behemoth.
Milton's present age is again an experiential darkness—of naval
warfare—but his backward glance to Satanic origins reveals the full
truth of which Homer, Virgil, Tasso give only incomplete reflec-
tions. Whether the transumption truly overcomes Spenser's Orgo-
glio is more dubious, for he remains nearly as Satanic as Milton's
Satan, except that Satan is more complex and poignant, being a
son of heaven and not, like the gross Orgoglio, a child of earth.

The third transumption of the passage, the fiction of the leaves,
is surely the subtlest, and the one most worthy of Milton's great-
ness. He tropes here on the tropes of Isaiah, Homer, Virgil and
Dante, and with the Orion allusion on Job and Virgil. The series
is capped by the references to Exodus and Ovid, with the equation
of Busiris and Satan. This movement from fallen leaves to starry
influence over storms to the overwhelming of a tyrannous host is it-
self a kind of transumption, as Milton moves from metonymy to
metonymy before accomplishing a final reduction.

Satan's fallen hosts, poignantly still called "angel forms," most
directly allude to a prophetic outcry of Isaiah 34:4:

And all the host of heaven shall be dissolved, and the heavens
shall be rolled together as a scroll; and all their host shall fall
down, as the leaf falleth off from the vine, and as a falling fig
from the fig tree.

Milton is too wary to mark this for transumption; his trope works upon a series of Homer, Virgil, Dante:

> . . . why ask of my generation?
> As is the generation of leaves, so is that of humanity.
> The wind scatters the leaves on the ground, but the fine timber
> burgeons with leaves again in the season of spring returning.
> So one generation of men will grow while another dies. . . .
> [*Iliad*, VI, 145-50, Lattimore version]

> thick as the leaves that with the early frost
> of autumn drop and fall within the forest,
> or as the birds that flock along the beaches,
> in flight from frenzied seas when the chill season
> drives them across the waves to lands of sun.
> They stand; each pleads to be the first to cross
> the stream; their hands reach out in longing for
> the farther shore. But Charon, sullen boatman,
> now takes these souls, now those; the rest he leaves;
> thrusting them back, he keeps them from the beach.
> [*Aeneid*, VI, 310-19; Mandelbaum version, 407-16]

. . . But those forlorn and naked souls changed color, their teeth chattering, as soon as they heard the cruel words. They cursed God, their parents, the human race, the place, the time, the seed of their begetting and of their birth. Then, weeping loudly, all drew to the evil shore that awaits every man who fears not God. The demon Charon, his eyes like glowing coals, beckons to them and collects them all, beating with his oar whoever lingers.

As the leaves fall away in autumn, one after another, till the bough sees all its spoils upon the ground, so there the evil seed of Adam: one by one they cast themselves from that shore at signals, like a bird at its call. Thus they go over the dark water, and before they have landed on the other shore, on this side a new throng gathers.

> [*Inferno*, III, 100-120, Singleton version]

Homer accepts grim process; Virgil accepts yet plangently laments, with his unforgettable vision of those who stretch forth their hands out of love for the farther shore. Dante, lovingly close to Virgil, is more terrible, since his leaves fall even as the evil seed of Adam falls. Milton remembers standing, younger and then able to see, in the woods at Vallombrosa, watching the autumn leaves strew the brooks. His characteristic metonymy of shades for woods allusively puns on Virgil's and Dante's images of the shades gathering for Charon, and by a metalepsis carries across Dante and Virgil to their tragic Homeric origin. Once again, the precursors are projected into belatedness, as Milton introjects the prophetic source of Isaiah. Leaves fall from trees, generations of men die, because once one-third of the heavenly host came falling down. Milton's present time again is experiential loss; he watches no more autumns, but the optic glass of his art sees fully what his precursors saw only darkly, or in the vegetable glass of nature.

By a transition to the "scattered sedge" of the Red Sea, Milton calls up Virgil again, compounding two passages on Orion:

> Our prows were pointed there when suddenly,
> rising upon the surge, stormy Orion
> drove us against blind shoals. . . .
>
> > [*Aeneid*, I, 534-36; Mandelbaum version, 753-55]

> . . . he marks Arcturus,
> the twin Bears and the rainy Hyades,
> Orion armed with gold; and seeing all
> together in the tranquil heavens, loudly
> he signals. . . .
>
> > [*Aeneid*, III, 517-21; Mandelbaum version, 674-78]

Alastair Fowler notes the contrast to the parallel Biblical allusions:

> He is wise in heart, and mighty in strength: who hath hardened himself against him, and hath prospered?
> . . . Which alone spreadeth out the heavens, and treadeth upon the waves of the sea.
> Which maketh Arcturus, Orion, and Pleiades, and the chambers of the south.
>
> > [Job 9:4, 8-9]

> Seek him that maketh the seven stars and Orion, and turneth the shadow of death into the morning, and maketh the day dark with night: that calleth for the waters of the sea, and poureth them out upon the face of the earth: The LORD is his name. . . .
>
> [Amos 5:8]

In Virgil, Orion rising marks the seasonal onset of storms. In the Bible, Orion and all the stars are put into place as a mere sign-system, demoted from their pagan status as powers. Milton says "hath vexed" to indicate that the sign-system continues in his own day, but he says "o'erthrew" to show that the Satanic stars and the host of Busiris the Pharaoh fell once for all, Pharaoh being a type of Satan. Virgil, still caught in a vision that held Orion as a potency, is himself again transumed into a sign of error.

I have worked through this passage's allusions in some detail so as to provide one full instance of a transumptive scheme in *Paradise Lost*. Johnson's insight is validated, for the "adventitious image" of the optic glass is shown to be not extrinsic at all, but rather to be the device that "crowds the imagination," compressing or hastening much transumption into a little space. By arranging his precursors in series, Milton figuratively reverses his obligation to them, for his stationing crowds them between the visionary truth of his poem (carefully aligned with Biblical truth) and his darkened present (which he shares with Galileo). Transumption murders time, for by troping on a trope, you enforce a state of rhetoricity or word-consciousness, and you negate fallen history. Milton does what Bacon hoped to do; Milton and Galileo become ancients, and Homer, Virgil, Ovid, Dante, Tasso, Spenser become belated moderns. The cost is a loss in the immediacy of the living moment. Milton's meaning is remarkably freed of the burden of anteriority, but only because Milton himself is already one with the future, which he introjects.

It would occupy too many pages to demonstrate another of Milton's transumptive schemes in its largest and therefore most powerful dimensions, but I will outline one, summarizing rather than quoting the text, and citing rather than giving the allusions. My motive is not only to show that the "optic glass" passage is hardly unique in its arrangement, but to analyze more thoroughly Milton's self-awareness of both his war against influence and his use of rhetoricity as a defense. Of many possibilities, Book I, lines 670-798, seems to me the best, for this concluding movement of the epic's initial book has as its hidden subject both the anxiety of influence and an anxiety of morality about the secondariness of any poetic creation, even Milton's own. The passage describes the sudden building, out of the deep, of Pandaemonium, the palace of Satan, and ends with the infernal peers sitting there in council.

This sequence works to transume the crucial precursors again—Homer, Virgil, Ovid and Spenser—but there are triumphant allusions here to Lucretius and Shakespeare also (as Fowler notes). In some sense, the extraordinary and reverberating power of the Pandaemonium masque (as John Hollander terms it, likening it to transformation scenes in court masques) depends on its being a continuous and unified allusion to the very idea of poetic tradition, and to the moral problematic of that idea. Metalepsis or transumption can be described as an extended trope with a missing or weakened middle, and for Milton literary tradition is such a trope. The illusionistic sets and complex machinery of the masque transformation scene are emblematic, in the Pandaemonium sequence, of the self-deceptions and morally misleading machinery of epic and tragic convention.

Cunningly, Milton starts the sequence with a transumption to the fallen near-present, evoking the royal army in the Civil War as precise analogue to the Satanic army. Mammon leads on the advance party, in an opening allusion to Spenser's Cave of Mammon canto, since both Mammons direct gold-mining operations. With the next major allusion, to the same passage in Ovid's *Metamorphoses* I that was evoked in the Galileo sequence, Milton probes the morality of art:

> Let none admire
> That riches grow in Hell; that soil may best
> Deserve the precious bane. And here let those
> Who boast in mortal things, and wond'ring tell
> Of *Babel*, and the works of *Memphian* Kings,
> Learn how thir greatest Monuments of Fame,
> And Strength and Art are easily outdone
> By Spirits reprobate, and in an hour
> What in an age they with incessant toil
> And hands innumerable scarce perform.

Milton presumably would not have termed the *Iliad* or the *Aeneid* "precious bane," yet the force of his condemnation extends to them, and his anxiety necessarily touches his own poem as well. Pandaemonium rises in baroque splendor, with a backward allusion to Ovid's Palace of the Sun, also designed by Mulciber (*Metamorphoses* II, 1-4), and with a near-contemporary allusion to St. Peter's at Rome and, according to Fowler, to Bernini's colonnade in the piazza of St. Peter's. Mulciber, archetype not only of Bernini but more darkly of all artists, including epic poets, becomes the center of the sequence:

> Men call'd him *Mulciber*; and how he fell
> From Heav'n, they fabl'd, thrown by angry *Jove*
> Sheer o'er the Crystal Battlements: from Morn
> To Noon he fell, from Noon to dewy Eve,
> A Summer's day; and with the setting Sun
> Dropt from the Zenith like a falling Star,
> On *Lemnos* th'*Ægæan* Isle: thus they relate,
> Erring; for he with this rebellious rout
> Fell long before; nor aught avail'd him now
> To have built in Heav'n high Towrs; nor did he scape
> By all his Engines, but was headlong sent
> With his industrious crew to build in hell.

The devastating "Erring" of line 747 is a smack at Homer by way of the *errat* of Lucretius (*De rerum natura*, I, 393, as Fowler notes). The contrast with Homer's passage illuminates the transumptive function of Milton's allusiveness, for Homer's Hephaistos (whose Latin name was Vulcan or Mulciber) gently fables his own downfall:

> . . . It is too hard to fight against the Olympian.
> There was a time once before now I was minded to help you,
> and he caught me by the foot and threw me from the magic threshold,
> and all day long I dropped helpless, and about sunset
> I landed in Lemnos. . . .
>
> [*Iliad*, I, 589-93; Lattimore version]

Milton first mocks Homer by over-accentuating the idyllic nature of this fall, and then reverses Homer completely. In the dark present, Mulciber's work is still done when the bad eminence of baroque glory is turned to the purposes of a fallen Church. So, at line 756, Pandaemonium is called "the high capital" of Satan, alluding to two lines of Virgil (*Aeneid*, VI, 836 and VIII, 348), but the allusion is qualified by the complex simile of the bees that continues throughout lines 768-75, and which relies on further allusions to *Iliad*, II, 87-90 and *Aeneid*, 430-36, where Achaian and Carthaginian heroes respectively are compared to bees. One of the most remarkable of Milton's transumptive returns to present time is then accomplished by an allusion to Shakespeare's *Midsummer Night's Dream*, II, i, 28ff. A "belated peasant" beholds the "Faery Elves" even as we, Milton's readers, see the giant demons shrink in size. Yet *our* belatedness is again redressed by metaleptic reversal, with an allusion to *Aeneid*, VI, 451-54, where Aeneas recognizes Dido's "dim shape among the shadows (just as one who either sees or thinks he sees . . . the moon rising)." So the belated peasant "sees, or dreams he sees" the elves, but like Milton we *know* we see the fallen angels metamorphosed from giants into pygmies. The Pandaemonium sequence ends with the great conclave of "a thousand demi-gods on golden seats," in clear parody of ecclesiastical assemblies re-convened after the Restoration. As with the opening reference to the advance-party of the royal army, the present is seen as fallen on evil days, but it provides vantage for Milton's enduring vision.

So prevalent throughout the poem is this scheme of allusion that any possibility of inadvertence can be ruled out. Milton's design is wholly definite, and its effect is to reverse literary tradition, at the expense of the presentness of the present. The precursors return in Milton, but only at his will, and they return to be corrected. Perhaps only Shakespeare can be judged Milton's rival in allusive triumph over tradition, yet Shakespeare had no Spenser to subsume, but only a Marlowe, and Shakespeare is less clearly in overt competition with Aeschylus, Sophocles, Euripides than Milton is with Homer, Virgil, Ovid, Dante, Tasso.

Hobbes, in his *Answer to Davenant's Preface* (1650), had subordinated wit to judgment, and so implied also that rhetoric was subordinate to dialectic:

> From knowing much, proceedeth the admirable variety and novelty of metaphors and similitudes, which are not possibly to be lighted on in the compass of a narrow knowledge. And the want whereof compelleth a writer to expressions that are either defaced by time or sullied with vulgar or long use. For the phrases of poesy, as the airs of music, with often hearing become insipid; the reader having no more sense of their force, than our flesh is sensible of the bones that sustain it. As the sense we have of bodies, consisteth in change and variety of impression, so also does the sense of language in the variety and changeable use of words. I mean not in the affectation of words newly brought home from travel, but in new (and withal, significant) translation to our purposes, of those that be already received, and in far fetched (but withal, apt, instructive, and comely) similitudes. . . .

Had Milton deliberately accepted this as challenge, he could have done no more both to fulfill and to refute Hobbes than *Paradise Lost* already does. What Davenant and Cowley could not

manage was a complete translation to their own purposes of re-
ceived rhetoric; but Milton raised such translation to sublimity. In
doing so, he also raised rhetoric over dialectic, *contra* Hobbes, for
his farfetchedness (Puttenham's term for transumption) gave simil-
itudes the status and function of complex arguments. Milton's
wit, his control of rhetoric, was again the exercise of the mind
through all her powers, and not a lower faculty subordinate to
judgment. Had Hobbes written his *Answer* twenty years later, and
after reading *Paradise Lost*, he might have been less confident of
the authority of philosophy over poetry.

8

In the shadow of Milton

Among the hills
He gazed upon that mighty orb of song,
The divine Milton.

               Wordsworth, The Excursion, *I, 248-50*

Milton is his great idol, and he sometimes dares to compare
himself with him.

               Hazlitt on Wordsworth

This chapter offers brief readings of four poems: Wordsworth's *Intimations* Ode, Shelley's *Ode to the West Wind*, Keats's *Ode to Psyche*, and Tennyson's *Ulysses*. Wordsworth's poem is written directly in the shadow of Milton, and may be called a misprision or powerful misreading of *Lycidas*. Shelley's poem is a strong misreading of Wordsworth's, while Keats's can be called a persuasive misinterpretation of several texts by both Milton and Wordsworth. Tennyson's dramatic monologue struggles with all four precursors, and marvelously achieves itself by one of the most complex misprisions in the language. All can be charted usefully and clearly on my map of misreading, and none has lost its disturbing power to affect the poetry of our own time. In Wallace Stevens alone, one can trace the effect of the *Intimations* Ode in a long sequence of poems from *Le Monocle de mon Oncle* to *The Auroras of Autumn*, while the *Ode to the West Wind* haunts a score of Stevens' poems, from *The Snow Man* through *Notes toward a Supreme Fiction* on to

Puella Parvula and *The Course of a Particular*. Similarly, the *Ode to Psyche* manifests itself in Stevens' *Credences of Summer* and *Ulysses* in Stevens' late *The Sail of Ulysses*. Parallel patterns of haunting can be discerned in Yeats and in the lesser poets of our century. Influence, in the deep sense, is a never-ending process.

Wordsworth's *Ode* traditionally has been analyzed as being in three parts: stanzas I-IV, V-VIII, and IX-XI. The first part begins with images of absence, the realm of: "There was a time." There is an *illusio* here, for though Wordsworth actually fears that a glory has passed away from himself, he says it has passed from the earth. As a defense, this reaction-formation wards off instinctual impulses by means of that mode of self-distrust that creates the superego. Poetically, instinctual impulses are internalized influences from a precursor-fixation, and Wordsworth's self-distrust reacts therefore to Milton's strength. "Intimations" in the title means something very like "signs" or "tokens," and the title therefore suggests that the poem is a searching for evidences, almost a quest for election. The precursor poem, in a deep sense, is Milton's *Lycidas*, and Wordsworth's *Ode* also is intended primarily to be a dedication to the poet's higher powers, a prolepsis of the great epic he hoped still to write. But that intention, though it will determine the poem's final attempt at a transumptive stand towards Milton, seems largely negated by much of the poem's first two movements.

It is important to see that images of absence dominate only the poem's first stanza, and the seven lines that close the fourth stanza, thus ending the first part. Most of the first four stanzas are given to images of natural presence, and the dialectical movement of these images, locked as they are between those of absence, is towards the ear rather than the eye. Wordsworth continues to hear with joy, though the deepest delight has abandoned his seeing. The joy of hearing restitutes, and provides the representing aspect of the poem's first movement, its noble synecdoche in which the image of the whole, the laughter of heaven and earth, replaces the image of the part, the poet's sense of loss in his seeing.

From stanzas V through VIII there are a series of images showing different aspects of emptying-out of a prior and valuable fullness. These include: trailing clouds, shades, journeyings westwards, fading of a greater into a lesser light, imitation of the lesser by the greater, darkness, and finally weighing down by frost. As images of reduction, they show subjectivity yielding to a world of things, of meaningless repetition, the "realistic" world of metonymies. This is Wordsworth's *kenosis*, his painful and gradual yielding-up of his own imaginative godhood, of his power of divination. Defensively, this pattern is of course a regression, but quite knowingly the defense is not successful. In stanza VIII, the power of repression provokes the imagery of the Sublime, alternating the image of the Child: "yet glorious in the might / Of heaven-born freedom on thy being's height" with the image of an even greater depth: "Heavy as frost, and deep almost as life!" The entire stanza is hyperbolic, straining at the limits of expression, as it addresses the little child as "best Philosopher," "mighty Prophet! Seer blest!"

By now it should be clear how closely Wordsworth's *Ode* sets or follows the patterns of our map of misreading. The poem's third movement begins with the long stanza IX, which concludes with the poem's major metaphor:

> Hence in a season of calm weather
> Though inland far we be,
> Our Souls have sight of that immortal sea
> Which brought us hither,
> Can in a moment travel thither,
> And see the Children sport upon the shore,
> And hear the mighty waters rolling evermore.

Much of stanza IX, before this passage, has turned on an imagistic perspectivism of inside against outside, which de Man has pointed to as the most characteristic variety of Romantic imagery. Wordsworth praises, as intimations of immortality, "obstinate questionings / Of sense and outward things." The poem's prime intimation of immortality is its metaphoric vision of the children and of the immortal sea. Are these inner or outer images? The perspectivism of the metaphor, with its "inland" resembling a deep region of consciousness, makes any reply problematic. It is the irony of perspectivism that it is as self-contradictory as a tautology is, peculiarly ironic since the original meaning of *perspicere* was "to see clearly." An individual point of view necessarily depends upon the Cartesian distinction between thinking subject and extended objects, and so dissolves knowing into subjectivity. We can observe that stanza IX, as a defense, is Wordsworth's sublimation of his deepest instincts, and like all sublimation it cannot suffice for a poem, for it too dissolves poetic divination and gives too little in return. Wordsworth can live more "normally" as a man by contenting himself with internal returns to his "oceanic sense," but can he go on living as a poet so strong as to challenge the desires of all poets who preceded him?

Stanzas X-XI move therefore to a final representation, in which metaphor is replaced by a metaleptic reversal or scheme of transumption. Richard Bernheimer, in his pioneering book *The Nature of Representation*, remarked that "representation . . . is a magical defense against time and the daemonic." Akin to this is Bronislaw Malinowski's general theory of magical language, in *Coral Gardens and Their Magic*, which describes the crucial words of Trobriand magic as "words of blessing, anticipatory affirmations of prosperity and plenty, exorcisms of evil influences, and mythological references which draw upon the strength of the past for the welfare of the future." What Bernheimer abstracts, and Malinowski observes in the Trobrianders, are lesser versions of Milton's mode of allusion that Wordsworth now adapts for his own purposes as he concludes his *Ode*.

The imagery of the two final stanzas juxtaposes an apparent acceptance of belatedness in stanza X with a revival of earliness in stanza XI, a revival that allusively contrasts its solar image with Milton's at the close of *Lycidas*. The acceptance of belatedness at first seems complete:

> What though the radiance which was once so bright
> Be now for ever taken from my sight,
>   Though nothing can bring back the hour
> Of splendour in the grass, of glory in the flower;
>   We will grieve not. . . .

But the final stanza proclaims freshness and earliness:

> The innocent brightness of a new-born Day
>   Is lovely yet. . . .

Lycidas ends with a contrast between Milton as "uncouth" or unknown swain, the ephebe, and the setting sun, which a few lines before has prefigured the resurrection of the drowned poet through the power of the resurrected Christ:

> So sinks the day-star in the ocean bed,
> And yet anon repairs his drooping head,
> And tricks his beams, and with new-spangled ore
> Flames in the forehead of the morning sky:
> So Lycidas sunk low, but mounted high,
> Through the dear might of him that walked the waves. . . .

But at the close the sun is only natural, and the ephebe recommencing his quest is at least as vulnerable as nature is:

> And now the sun had stretched out all the hills,
> And now was dropped into the western bay;
> At last he rose, and twitched his mantle blue:
> Tomorrow to fresh woods, and pastures new.

Wordsworth, with an eye on these passages, transumes Milton:

> The clouds that gather round the setting sun
> Do take a sober colouring from an eye
> That hath kept watch o'er man's mortality;
> Another race hath been, and other palms are won.

The Wordsworth of the *Ode* will not present himself as an "uncouth swain," and the sober coloring imparted by his mature eye substitutes for the blue of the Miltonic mantle. Keeping watch over mortality does not mean yielding to it, wholly, and "another race" means perhaps the race in *Areopagitica*, "where that immortal garland is to be run for, not without dust and heat." Wordsworth has sallied out and lovingly seen his adversary in the race, Milton, but the transumptive "other palms" are not a convincing substitute for the garland that intimates poetic immortality. Still, by his defensive images, Wordsworth at least has attempted a projection of the past, however glorious it was, and an introjection of the future, though sorrowfully that was to fail him. But the revisionary design of his Great Ode in any case has triumphed, for versions of it are with us still.

Overwhelmingly, Wordsworth's poem is the angel with whom Shelley wrestles in his *Ode to the West Wind*, where the tripartite structure appears as: stanzas I-III, *clinamen/tessera*; IV, *kenosis/daemonization*; V, *askesis/apophrades*. Shelley had written an earlier misprision of *Intimations* in his *Hymn to Intellectual Beauty*, a poem that barely deviates from the Wordsworthian model. Three years later, Shelley is a far bolder revisionist, as he watches another sunset and reflects on his own fears that there are no more palms to be won, at least not by a failed prophet like himself. As a spent seer, Shelley consigns order to the wind as vehicle of change, but he will reclaim much of that order before his poem ends.

The wind as "unseen presence" is necessarily the dominant image of the entire poem, but it blows most dialectically as "destroyer and preserver" throughout the first three stanzas. As the wind drives on, the presences of earth, sky and sea are revealed as being mostly absences. From the start, Shelley ironically reacts against the Wordsworthian sober coloring, with the "yellow, and black, and pale, and hectic red" of his dead leaves. The central irony of the first three stanzas is that the wind, as enchanter or exorcist, is itself the reason why nothing, including Shelley, is in its right place, though in Shelley's instance this is because inspiration has made him an outcast prophet. Shelley is defending himself against his own interpretation of Wordsworth's account of imaginative loss being transformed into experiential gain, an interpretation that sees poets, like ocean foliage, trembling and despoiling themselves of their own imaginative powers.

Throughout these stanzas, the restituting synecdoche is in the microcosm of the wind's actions, again both as destroyer (political revolution) and as preserver (resurrection in the apocalypse). The disturbance of leaves, clouds, waves is a part of the greater disturbance to come. As defense, Shelley reverses into the opposite, but more dangerously turns his destructive impulses against himself, with consequences more evident in stanza IV.

One critical advantage of our map can be seen in the clarity of contrast it gives us between stanzas IV and V of the poem. Shelley empties out his poetic self in stanza IV, regressing ("If even / I were as in my boyhood") and metonymically isolating himself in his famous prayer for reduction: "Oh, lift me as a wave, a leaf, a cloud!" From this *kenosis* he reacts through one of the most famous and misunderstood hyperboles in the language:

> I fall upon the thorns of life! I bleed!

> A heavy weight of hours has chained and bowed
> One too like thee: tameless, and swift, and proud.

Keats, in line 245 of *Sleep and Poetry*, had implied an attack upon Byron (probably), and Shelley (possibly), when he said that poetic strength alone was not enough, "for it feeds upon the burrs, / And thorns of life." Shelley alludes also to the closing lines of stanza VIII of the *Intimations* Ode with their similar image of heaviness. The poet's hyperbolic fall, though it follows in a tradition of the defense we have learned to call repression, takes place because what he attempts to repress is too strong to stay down: tamelessness, swiftness of spirit, pride.

The strength of any rebellion is in its own implicit patterning, the form that is its force. As in a larger work like *Prometheus Unbound*, Shelley rebels against Wordsworth and Milton in his ode, yet the form of the rebellion belongs to the precursors. Where Wordsworth began the third movement of *Intimations* with a sublimating image of "embers," Shelley concludes with "ashes and sparks," his version of "something that doth live." The major sublimating image is Shelley's transformation of the inside/outside metaphor endemic in Romanticism:

> Make me thy lyre, even as the forest is:
> What if my leaves are falling like its own!
> The tumult of thy mighty harmonies
>
> Will take from both a deep, autumnal tone,
> Sweet though in sadness. . . .

The "deep, autumnal tone" alludes both to *Intimations'* "sober coloring" and to *Tintern Abbey*'s "still, sad music," but Shelley associates this appeal to "primal sympathy" with a failed metaphor, here of the poet as Aeolian harp. The metaphor's limitations culminate in the vainly anguished prayers "Be thou, Spirit fierce, / My spirit! Be thou me, impetuous one!" where the inner and the outer, poet and west wind, fall away from one another even as the poet begs for union. It is in the final eight lines that the at least partly saving representation comes, as the belated poet becomes a prophet after all and concludes with a transumptive rather than a rhetorical question:

> Be through my lips to unawakened earth
>
> The trumpet of a prophecy! O, Wind,
> If Winter comes, can Spring be far behind?

The prophecy is *not* being uttered in the present moment, which is after all the coming of Autumn; the present moment has gone out of the poem, even as it vanished in Milton's kind of serial allusiveness. Spring literally is six months behind, but Shelley tropes upon a trope, and his introjection of the future hints at his answer. The Miltonic "pastures new" and the Wordsworthian "meanest flower that blows" are seen alike as parts only of "unawakened earth" as Shelley joins himself to Jeremiah's prophetic cry: "O earth, earth, earth, hear the word of the LORD." Neither Christian hope nor natural sympathy will suffice, but Shelley offers in their place "the incantation of this verse," his own word-consciousness perhaps, yet touched to Isaiah's "live coal" by a great revisionist's art.

Shelley was a natural revisionist, by intellect and temperament. Keats, though pugnacious, was not a polemicist, and can be judged to have become a revisionist entirely because of the necessities of a purely poetic misprision. The first of his great odes, the *Ode to Psyche*, takes belatedness as its overt subject and struggles with the shadows of Milton and Wordsworth, but not to win a blessing, as Shelley does. Keats is concerned rather with clearing an imaginative space for himself, in the hope of finding a map with blanks that he himself can fill in. But his one resource, like Wordsworth's, is further internalization, which condemns him to a fairly strict following of the map of misprision. A brief, digressive meditation on internalization is necessary, if the overcoming of obstacles first by Keats, and then by Tennyson following after him, is to be justly appreciated.

Internalization of the precursor is the ratio I have called *apophrades*, and in psychoanalysis it is hardly distinguishable from introjection. To trope upon a trope is to internalize it, so that aesthetic internalization seems very close to the kind of allusiveness that Milton perfected, the Romantics inherited, and Joyce brought to a new perfection in our century. Yet conflicts can be internalized also, and the Freudian theory of the superego seems dependent upon the notion that a father's authority can be internalized by the superego. Romantic internalization, as I have shown in another study, "The Internalization of Quest Romance," takes place primarily in intra-subjective terms, the conflict being between opposing principles *within the ego*. Further internalization, then, may aid in freeing a poet from superego-anxieties (the constraints perhaps of religious or moral tradition) or from ambivalence towards himself, but it is not of any initiatory use as a defense against precursors or id-anxieties, though it does enter into the final phase of the influence-struggle. Keats, who programmatically internalizes his themes in the *Ode to Psyche* and afterwards, is therefore peculiarly and overtly conscious of the anxiety of influence, even for a strong poet of the second Romantic generation. I suspect that is why the *Ode to Psyche*, a profoundly self-discovering poem, follows the map of misprision more rigorously than all but a few other poems. Each of *Psyche*'s first four stanzas emphasizes one ratio in turn, with the fifth and last stanza dividing almost equally between the two final ratios. Keats does not displace his Miltonic-Wordsworthian model in any formal way, but relies entirely upon finding fresh imaginative space within himself.

The gently ironic opening stanza seems at first directed against the start of *Lycidas*, and certainly Keats's high good humor is maintained throughout; but the irony is a personal defense also. Keats gives us images of a surprising presence, of a Psyche "wingèd" and so divine, yet also re-united with Cupid here upon earth. But allusiveness is internalized in this opening *illusio*, and Keats hints that his role as *voyeur* is surprisingly close to that of Milton's Satan. He "Saw two fair creatures, couchèd side by side," just as Satan saw how our first parents "Straight side by side were laid, nor turn'd I ween / Adam from his fair Spouse . . . ," and just as the angel Gabriel some fifty lines later told his subordinates to "leave unsearcht no nook / But chiefly where those two fair Creatures lodge. . . ." In some sense Keats says Cupid and Psyche but means Adam and Eve; and in some sense he condemns himself for sharing Satan's lust of the eye, though again the self-condemnation is surely not wholly serious.

But the poetic dilemma is quite serious. Psyche is a belated god-

dess, and Keats is a belated poet, which is why the synecdoche of
the second stanza culminates in so excited a recognition of Psyche,
for this is also a moment of poetic self-recognition in which Keats
discovers his true muse, though in a gently idealized form, not the
grandly purgatorial form she will assume as Moneta in *The Fall of
Hyperion*. The reunited lovers, Cupid and Psyche, are an image of
the wholeness that Keats's mature poetry will seek.

In the next stanza, Keats reduces mythology to a metonymic cat-
alog of emptiness, and though the reduction is remarkably light in
tone, it has a defensive element nevertheless, for its motive is to
deprecate poetic earliness, through the process of isolation. From
so good-natured a nadir, one might not expect a strongly daemonic
recovery to rise, yet Keats does achieve a Sublime of brightness un-
til he can utter the wonderful hyperbole: "I see, and sing, by my
own eyes inspired." With the single change of "no" to "thy" he
proceeds to rescue the particulars of mythological worship from the
fragmentary discontinuity into which he had broken them in the
previous stanza:

> So let me be thy choir, and make a moan
>   Upon the midnight hours;
> Thy voice, thy lute, thy pipe, thy incense sweet
>   From swingèd censer teeming;
> Thy shrine, thy grove, thy oracle, thy heat
>   Of pale-mouthed prophet dreaming.

The heightening here is conveyed more through intensity of tone
than through image, but the defense of repression is so finely ob-
vious as to make commentary redundant. In the metaphor that fol-
lows, the familiar Romantic conceit of an internalized nature al-
most transcends its perspectivizing limitations, so extraordinary is
Keats's art:

> Yes, I will be thy priest, and build a fane
>   In some untrodden region of my mind,

Where branchèd thoughts, new grown with pleasant pain,
   Instead of pines shall murmur in the wind:
Far, far around shall those dark-clustered trees
   Fledge the wild-ridgèd mountains steep by steep;
And there by zephyrs, streams, and birds, and bees,
   The moss-lain Dryads shall be lulled to sleep. . . .

Internalization has taken him where he has not been before, and
it is always a surprise to realize that this landscape, and this oxymo-
ronic intensity, are wholly inside his psyche. The landscape is
Wordsworthian, and the sublimation of a surrendered outside na-
ture would seem to be complete, particularly with the beautiful but
defeated image of the wood nymphs reclining on banks of moss, a
pastoral sensuality that by being altogether mental suggests a real-
istic erotic despair. Keats completes the poem with a superb rhet-
oricity that substitutes for the earlier refrain of "too late," yet does
so all too knowingly to be self-deceived:

And in the midst of this wide quietness
A rosy sanctuary will I dress
With the wreathed trellis of a working brain,
   With buds, and bells, and stars without a name,
With all the gardener Fancy e'er could feign,
   Who breeding flowers, will never breed the same:
And there shall be for thee all soft delight
   That shadowy thought can win,
A bright torch, and a casement ope at night,
   To let the warm Love in!

There is past time here, in the anterior feignings of the gardener
Fancy, and there is a promised future, where Keats may substitute
himself for the warm Cupid, but clearly there is no present time
whatsoever. Keats projects the past as feigning and introjects the
future as love, but even as there is no present moment so there is
no place of presence, nor perhaps will there ever be. The Words-
worthian "wide quietness" and "shadowy thought" allude to the
"shadowy ground" of man's mind that Wordsworth had pro-

claimed as the main region of his song in the *Recluse* fragment, part of which Keats had read as the "Prospectus" to *The Excursion*. What does Keats promise his Psyche? An earliness to wed her earliness, a bright torch to match her "brightest" that began the fourth stanza; but what is the reality of such earliness? Keats honestly gives only to take away, for how soft a delight can shadowy thought win? The open casement, as in line 69 of the *Ode to a Nightingale*, is the genuine promise of earliness, and yet here as there it alludes transumptively to the Spenserian world of romance. Few poems are as persuasive as the *Ode to Psyche* is in its interpretation of its precursors; and few poems know so much about themselves and are able to complete themselves despite such knowledge.

I end this chapter with an heroic knower, Tennyson's Ulysses, whose dramatic monologue, akin to Childe Roland's, I read as the belated strong poet's act of judgment upon Romantic tradition, as well as upon himself. In some sense, Tennyson's Ulysses is the Romantic quester grown old and perfect in his solipsism, a Childe Harold who has lived too long and now secretly loathes his own belatedness. Unlike Roland, he is anything but a failure, yet his own fame tortures his inactivity. It may be that the discordant qualities of this Ulysses, at once a genuine seeker after heroic knowledge and an unloving egomaniac, are reconcilable within the context of misprision, with all its attendant ambivalences. Time is the Romantic antagonist, not, as Nietzsche thought, language. Ulysses, like Childe Roland, cannot both know and love, for these are antithetical to one another in a world too consciously late. Kant's remark that art is purposiveness without purpose is as applicable to this Ulysses as to Childe Roland. Of the two, Ulysses is the closer to nihilism but the less demoniac and so more immediately acceptable by the reader, though one would no more want to be in one boat with him than one would want to be riding by Roland's side.

Ulysses opens both with a complex and a simple irony, but only the simpler one, irony as figure of speech, is of structural importance. The speaker's own bitterness is complex and overt, irony as figure of thought, and has no defensive function. But the defensive irony is the *illusio*, in which Ulysses says "idle king" but means what we would call a "responsible" one, busy with *others* and not with the internalized quest of knowing his own greatness. When he says he cannot rest from travel, he means what all the great solipsists driven to exploration mean, that he cannot rest until he is left alone with himself. His truest and largest ancestor is Milton's Satan in Book II of *Paradise Lost*, where the Grand Solipsist becomes the first and the greatest explorer, moving through a Chaos that accurately mirrors his soul. So Ulysses speaks of his own greatness, both in enjoyment and suffering, and "both with those / That loved me, and alone." Is there a difference? Nowhere in the poem does he speak of *his* loving anyone else, and we may interpret his sense of his own greatness as being the only synecdochal representation of which he is capable: "I am a part of all that I have met." For so godlike a consciousness, *kenosis* is a terrible emptiness, and the defense of undoing an almost perpetual process. Ulysses himself says, with pride but also knowing the price: "I am become a name," or a wandering metonymy, a cataloger of both the self and everything lying outside the self. He is "always roaming with a *hungry* heart" because his heart is always empty, and no quantity of things "seen and known" can fill it up. His perpetually receding horizon is simply an endlessly regressive process, a compulsive repetition, which is doubtless heroic, but makes us both admire and protest his remarkable murmur "As though to breathe were life." It is not the worst part of us, necessarily, that wants to answer back: "To breathe is also to live." But we are not Sublime questers, and we yield to his subsequent *daemonization*, the high passion of his power of repression:

> Life piled on life
> Were all too little, and of one to me
> Little remains: but every hour is saved
> From that eternal silence, something more,

A bringer of new things; and vile it were
For some three suns to store and hoard myself,
And this grey spirit yearning in desire
To follow knowledge like a sinking star,
Beyond the utmost bound of human thought.

What the map of misprision helps us to see is the compulsive
desperation of this heroic hyperbole, as no height will suffice his
need, even if he had life to pile upon life. "The utmost bound of
human thought" begins to seem like a wisdom that Ulysses, like
Satan, is not capable of learning.

For so desperately strenuous a sensibility, the perspectivism of
metaphor is a perpetual sublimation that can never even begin to
work, any more than it could work for Satan. It is fascinating that
when the metaphor becomes overt, the inside/outside juxtaposition
emerges in the inescapable accents of Keats, Tennyson's prime
precursor:

Death closes all: but something ere the end,
Some work of noble note, may yet be done,
Not unbecoming men that strove with Gods.
The lights begin to twinkle from the rocks:
The long day wanes: the slow moon climbs: the deep
Moans round with many voices. . . .

Great word-painter that he is, following Keats, Tennyson offers
up his art in sublimation through the expiring gesture of his
quester's suicidal, final voyage. But the reader is likely to be moved
less by this failed limitation than by the marvelously transumptive
representation that substitutes for it and grandly ends the poem, in
the accents of Milton's Satan at his most equivocally glorious:

Though much is taken, much abides; and though
We are not now that strength which in old days
Moved earth and heaven; that which we are, we are;
One equal temper of heroic hearts,

Made weak by time and fate, but strong in will
To strive, to seek, to find, and not to yield.

When is "now" for a Ulysses about to voyage forth again? It exists only until the speaker can abandon it, for by "old days" he means earlier or younger days, that is, "old days" is a figure of a figure. The past has been projected and is cast out into age, and the present rushes forth into the future, introjecting the endless earliness that Ulysses must have if he is to go on knowing himself as strong. What is he then but another belated version of that aspect of Milton's Satan that is an allegory of the dilemma of the modern strong poet? Satan cries out for "courage never to submit or yield," and Ulysses will strive, seek, find (what, besides himself?) but most of all will not yield. Only a few steps on, and Stevens transumptively alludes to Tennyson's quester in *The Sail of Ulysses*, where Ulysses starts out by saying "As I know, I am and have / The right to be." This Ulysses seeks to receive "A divination, a letting down / Resolved in dazzling discovery." The strong poet, battling too strongly against his own belatedness, may be reduced by the necessities of misprision to the state described by Stevens in *The Poems of Our Climate*, where the defense of isolation is seen as having failed, and where the poet remains an "evilly compounded, vital I" that cannot be saved by transumption, by being "made . . . fresh in a world of white." The shadow in Stevens is more that of Emerson, as the American Milton, and the shadow too is perpetually made fresh.

9

Emerson and influence

Wallace Stevens, closing *It Must Change*, the second part of *Notes Toward a Supreme Fiction*, proclaimed the "will to change, a necessitous / And present way, a presentation" that brings about "the freshness of transformation." But though this transformation "is ourselves," the Seer of Hartford was too wily not to add a customary qualification:

> And that necessity and that presentation
> Are rubbings of a glass in which we peer.
> Of these beginnings, gay and green, propose
> The suitable amours. Time will write them down.

Stevens died in 1955, and many suitable amours concerning various beginnings have been proposed since then. Pound, Eliot, Williams, Moore are gone, among other major figures; and Crane and Roethke were ended prematurely in a subsequent generation. Jarrell and Berryman, whose achievements were more equivocal, have taken on some of the curious lustre that attends the circumstances of such deaths. Contemporary American poetry is a more than usually elaborate panorama, replete with schools and programs, with followers enough for all, and readers available for only a few. Even the best of our contemporary poets, whether of any grouping or of none, suffer a burden wholly appropriate to the valley of vision they

hope to have chosen, a burden more important finally than the im-
mediate sorrows of poetic over-population and the erosion of a lit-
erate audience. Peering in the glass of vision, contemporary poets
confront their too-recent giant precursors staring back at them, in-
ducing a profound anxiety that hides itself, but cannot be evaded
totally. The partial evasions of this anxiety can be identified simply
as the styles and strategies of contemporary verse, despite the overt
manifestos to the contrary at which current poets seem more than
usually adept. The anxiety of influence, a melancholy at a failure
in imaginative priority, still rages like the dog-star in recent poetry,
with the results that Pope observed. Poetically, call ours the Age of
Sirius, the actual cultural equivalent of the fictive counter-cultural
Age of Aquarius:

> The dog-star rages! nay 'tis past a doubt,
> All Bedlam, or Parnassus, is let out:
> Fire in each eye, and papers in each hand,
> They rave, recite, and madden round the land.

I write these pages after passing an educational hour watching
an array of revolutionary bards, black and white, chanting on tele-
vision. Their exhilarating apparent freedom from the anxiety of in-
fluence does not render even the most inchoate rhapsodes free of so
necessitous a malady. Mixed into the tide of rhetoric came the rec-
ognizable detritus of the precursors, ranging from the American
Sublime of Whitman to the sublime bathos of the Imamu Baraka,
yet containing some surprises—of Edna Millay shining clear in a
black poetess, or of Edgar Guest in a revolutionary balladeer, or of
Ogden Nash in a particularly ebullient open-former.

If we move to the other extreme of contemporary achievement,
say Ashbery's *Fragment* or Ammons' *Saliences*, then we confront,
as readers, far more intense cases of the anxiety of influence, for
Ashbery and Ammons, and a few others in their generation, have
matured into strong poets. Their best work, like Roethke's or Eliza-
beth Bishop's, begins to demand the same immense effort of the

whole being to absorb and resist as is required by the strongest American poets born in the last three decades of the nineteenth century: Robinson, Frost, Stevens, Pound, Moore, Williams, Eliot, Aiken, Ransom, Jeffers, Cummings, Crane. Perhaps no single reader greatly admires all of these dozen—I do not—but the work seems to abide, admired or not. Pound and Williams primarily, Stevens more recently, Frost and Eliot now rather less, have been the principal influences upon American poets born in the twentieth century, but all of these twelve poets have descendants, and all of them induce massive anxieties of influence, though the Pound-Williams schools (there are clearly several) emulate their precursors by a remarkable (and damaging) overt refusal to recognize such anxieties. Still, poets have joined in denying these anxieties for three hundred years now at least, even as they more and more strongly manifest them in their poems.

The war of American poets against influence is part of our Emersonian heritage, manifested first in the great triad of "The Divinity School Address," "The American Scholar," and "Self-Reliance." This heritage can be traced in Thoreau, Whitman, Dickinson and quite directly again in Robinson and Frost, in the architectural writings of Sullivan and Wright, in the *Essays Before a Sonata* of Charles Ives. The less direct heritage is more relevant to any brooding on the negative aspects of poetic influence, centering partly on Pound and Williams (where it is refracted through Whitman) and partly on Stevens, who disliked the very idea of influence.

This distaste is a proper characteristic of all Modern (meaning Post-Enlightenment or Romantic) poets, but peculiarly so of American poets coming after our prophet (however now unhonored) Emerson. I like Charles Ives' remark upon Emerson's ambitions: "His essay on the pre-soul (which he did not write) treats of that part of the over-soul's influence on unborn ages, and attempts the impossible only when it stops attempting it." Call Emerson the over-soul, and then contemplate his influence upon American poets who had read him (like Jeffers) and those who had not, yet read him in his poetic descendants (like Crane, who read his Emerson in Whitman). It can be called the only poetic influence that counsels against itself, and against the idea of influence. Perhaps in consequence, it has been the most pervasive of American poetic influences, though partly unrecognized. In nineteenth-century America, it operated as much by negation (Poe, Melville, Hawthorne), as by discipleship (Thoreau, Very, Whitman) or by a dialectical blend of the two relations (Dickinson, Tuckerman, the Jameses).

In a Journal entry (21 July 1837) Emerson recorded an insight that made possible his three anti-influence orations-essays of 1837-40:

> Courage consists in the conviction that they with whom you contend are no more than you. If we believed in the existence of strict *individuals*, natures, that is, not radically identical but unknown[,] immeasurable, we should never dare to fight.

This striking use of "individuals" manifests Emerson's acute apprehension of the sorrows of poetic influence, even as he declines to share these sorrows. If the new poet succumbs to a vision of the precursor as the Sublime, "unknown, immeasurable," then the great contention with the dead father will be lost. We can remember such ambivalent titans of intra-textuality as the quasi–nature deity Wordsworth of the later nineteenth century, and in our time that Gnostic divinity, Yeats, and our own current daemon of the American Sublime, Stevens. Emerson, shrewdest of all visionaries, early perceived the accurate enemy in the path of aspiring youth: "Genius is always sufficiently the enemy of genius by over-influence."

Though we rightly blame Emerson for our capitalistic reactionaries as well as for our shamanistic revolutionaries, for the whole range that goes from Henry Ford to the Whole Earth Catalog, his own meditations forestall our observations. His broodings against influence, starting in 1837, took their origins in the great business depression of that year. Confronting individualism in its terrible freedom, Emerson developed a characteristic antithetical notion of the individual: "Every man is an infinitely repellent orb, and holds his individual being on that condition." Most remarkably, the journal-meditations move to a great self-recognition on May 26, 1837:

> Who shall define to me an Individual? I behold with awe & delight many illustrations of the One Universal Mind. I see my being imbedded in it. As a plant in the earth so I grow in God. I am only a form of him. He is the soul of Me. I can even with a mountainous aspiring say, *I am God*, by transferring my *Me* out of the flimsy & unclean precinct of my body, my fortunes, my private will. . . . Yet why not always so? How came the Individual thus armed and impassioned to parricide thus murderously inclined ever to traverse & kill the divine life? Ah wicked Manichee! Into that dim problem I cannot enter. A believer in Unity, a seer of Unity, I yet behold two. . . .

The enormous split here is central in Emerson, pervades his conflicting ideas of influence, and is as relevant to contemporary poets as it was to Whitman, Robinson, Stevens, Crane, Roethke. Turning off the television set, I open the Sunday book supplement of the newspaper to behold a letter from Joyce Carol Oates, novelist, poet, critic, that replies to a reviewer:

> It is a fallacy of our time, hopefully coming to an end, that "individuals" are competitive and what one does lessens possibilities for another. . . . I believe that some day . . . all this wasteful worrying about who owns what, who "owns" a portion of art, will be finished. . . . In America, we need to get back to Whitman as our spiritual father, to write novels of the kind that might have grown out of "Leaves of Grass." Whitman understood that human beings are not really in competition, excluded from one another. He knew that the role of the poet is to "transfigure" and "clarify"—and, in that way, sanctify. . . .

This moving passage, by an ambitious ephebe of Dreiser, is indeed in Whitman's tradition, and so also in Emerson's. The over-idealization of literature here is normal and necessary for *the writer in a writer*, a self constrained to deny its own selfhood. So Blake grandly noted, after reading Wordsworth, that "this is all in the highest degree Imaginative and equal to any Poet but not Superior. I cannot think that Real Poets have any competition. None are greatest in the Kingdom of Heaven it is so in Poetry." Critics, who are people in search of images for acts of *reading,* and not of writing, have a different burden, and ought to cease emulating poets in the over-idealization of poetry.

Blake would have insisted that only the Spectre of Urthona, and not the "Real Man the Imagination" in him, experienced anxiety in reading Wordsworth or in reading their common father, Milton. Blakean critics, like Frye, too easily join Blake in this insistence. But this is not the critic's proper work, to take up the poet's stance. Perhaps there *is* a power or faculty of the Imagination, and certainly all poets *must* go on believing in its existence, but a critic makes a better start by agreeing with Hobbes that imagination is "decaying sense" and that poetry is written by the same natural man or woman who suffers daily all the inescapable anxieties of competition. This is not to say that the imagination refers to a world of things, but rather that a poet's consciousness of a competing poet is itself a text.

Emerson set out to excel "in Divinity," by which he meant, from the start, "eloquence," to the lasting scandal of certain American moralists from Andrews Norton to Yvor Winters; for Emerson was very much in the Oral Tradition, unlike his nearest contemporary equivalent, Nietzsche. Emerson tells his notebook, on April 18, 1824, a month before his twenty-first birthday: "I cannot dissemble that my abilities are below my ambition . . . ," but he cheerfully adds, "What we ardently love we learn to imitate," and so he hopes "to put on eloquence as a robe." Certainly he did, and he learned therefore the first meaning of his idea of Self-Reliance: "Every man has his own voice, manner, eloquence. . . ." He goes on to speak of each person's "sort of love and grief and imagination and action," but these are afterthoughts. The American orator-poet requires singularity in "voice, manner, eloquence," and if he has that, he trusts he has all, or almost all.

The primary Emerson is this confident orator, who as late as 1839 can still say, in his journals, that "it is the necessity of my nature to shed all influences." Mixed into this primary strain is a yearning *to be influenced*, but only by a Central Man who is yet to come. In 1845, a year before his Bacchic intensity of reaction against the Mexican War, Emerson characteristically began those expectations of a new man-god that emerged more fully in 1846. In the 1845 Journals, the tone might be called the apocalyptic wistful:

> We are candidates, we know we are, for influences more subtle and more high than those of talent and ambition. We want a leader, we want a friend whom we have not seen. In the company and fired by the example of a god, these faculties that dream and toss in their sleep would wake. Where is the Genius that shall marshal us the way that we were going? There is a vast residue, an open account ever.
>
> The great inspire us: how they beckon, how they animate, and show their legitimate power in nothing more than their power to misguide us. For the perverted great derange and deject us, and perplex ages with their fame. . . . This is that which the strong genius works upon; the region of destiny, of aspiration, of the unknown. . . .

We might follow Nietzsche, Emerson's admirer, and note that as Apollo apparently represents each new poet's individuation, so Dionysus ought to be emblematic of each poet's return to his subsuming precursors. Some such realization informed Emerson's dilemma, for he believed that poetry came only from Dionysian influx, yet he preached an Apollonian Self-Reliance while fearing the very individuation it would bring. "If only he *sees*, the world will be visible enough," is one Emersonian formula carrying this individuation to the borders of a sublime solipsism. Here, expounding nature's supposed method, is a greater formula:

His health and greatness consist in his being the channel through which heaven flows to earth, in short, in the fulness in which an ecstatical state takes place in him. It is pitiful to be an artist, when by forbearing to be artists we might be vessels filled with the divine overflowings, enriched by the circulations of omniscience and omnipresence. Are there not moments in the history of heaven when the human race was not counted by individuals, but was only the Influenced, was God in distribution, God rushing into multiform benefit? It is sublime to receive, sublime to love, but this lust of imparting as from *us*, this desire to be loved, the wish to be recognized as individuals,—is finite, comes of a lower strain.

Emerson's beautiful confusion *is* beautiful because the conflict is emotional, between equal impulses, and because it cannot be resolved. Influx would make us Bacchic, but *not* individuated poets; Self-Reliance will help make us poets, but "of a lower strain," short of ecstatic possession. Emerson's relative failure as a writer of verse ("failure" only when measured against his enormous basic aspirations) is caused by this conflict, and so is his over-valuation of poetry, *a poetry never yet written*, as he too frequently complains. He asks for a stance simultaneously Dionysiac and self-reliant, and he does not know how this is to be attained, nor do we. I suggest that the deeper cause for his impossible demand is his inner division on the burden of influx, at once altogether to be desired and yet altogether to be resisted, if it comes to us (as it must) from a precursor no more ultimately Central than ourselves, no less a text than we are.

But this is not just the native strain in Emerson; it is the American burden. It came to him because, at the right time in our cultural history, he bravely opened himself to it, but by opening to it with so astonishing a receptivity to oppositions, he opened all subsequent American artists to the same irreconcilable acceptance of negations. Post-Emersonian American poetry, when compared to post-Wordsworthian British poetry, or post-Goethean German poetry, or French poetry after Hugo, is uniquely open to influencings, and uniquely resistant to all *ideas* of influence. From Whitman to our contemporaries, American poets eagerly proclaim that they reject nothing that is best in past poetry, and as desperately succumb to poetic defense mechanisms, or self-malformings, rhetorical tropes run wild, against a crippling anxiety of influence. Emerson, source of our sorrow, remains to be quarried, not so much for a remedy, but for a fuller appreciation of the malady. The crux of the matter is a fundamental question for American poets. It could be phrased: In becoming a poet, is one joining oneself to a company of others or truly becoming a solitary and single one? In a sense, this is the anxiety of *whether* one ever really *became* a poet, a double anxiety: Did one truly join that company? Did one become truly oneself?

In his essay *Character*, Emerson emphasized the fear of influence:

> Higher natures overpower lower ones by affecting them with a certain sleep. The faculties are locked up, and offer no resistance. Perhaps that is the universal law. When the high cannot bring up the low to itself, it benumbs it, as man charms down the resistance of the lower animals. Men exert on each other a similar occult power. How often has the influence of a true master realized all the tales of magic! A river of command seemed to run down from his eyes into all those who beheld him, a torrent of strong sad light, like an Ohio or Danube, which pervaded them with his thoughts and colored all events with the hue of his mind.

This flood of light, which Emerson taught his descendants to fear, rather curiously ran down upon them from *his* eyes. As he himself said, in the essay *Politics*: "The boundaries of personal influence it is impossible to fix, as persons are organs of moral or supernatural force." Property, he cunningly added, had the same power. As eloquence, to Emerson, was identical with personal energy, eloquence was necessarily personal property, and the dialectics of energy became the dialectics also of commerce. One can say that for Emerson the imagination *was* linguistic energy.

At his most apocalyptic, as throughout the troubling year 1846, when he wrote his best poems, Emerson again denied the anxiety of influence, as here in "Uses of Great Men" from *Representative Men:*

> We need not fear excessive influence. A more generous trust is permitted. Serve the great. Stick at no humiliation. Grudge no office thou canst render. Be the limb of their body, the breath of their mouth. Compromise thy egotism. Who cares for that, so thou gain aught wider and nobler? Never mind the taunt of Boswellism: the devotion may easily be greater than the wretched pride which is guarding its own skirts. Be another: not thyself, but a Platonist; not a soul, but a Christian; not a naturalist, but a Cartesian; not a poet, but a Shakespearian. In vain, the wheels of tendency will not stop, nor will all the forces of inertia, fear, or of love itself hold thee there. On, and forever onward!

Though this over-protests, it remains haunted by the unfulfillable maxim: "Never imitate." Has Emerson forgotten his own insight, that one must be an inventor to read well? Whatever "we" means, in his passage, it cannot mean what it meant in a great notebook passage behind *Self-Reliance:* "We are a vision." Rather than multiply bewildering instances, of Emerson on all sides of this dark and central idea, we do him most justice by seeking his ultimate balance where always that must be sought, in his grandest essay, *Experience.* Solve this, and you have Emerson-on-influence, if he can be solved at all:

> Thus inevitably does the universe wear our color, and every object fall successively into the subject itself. The subject exists, the subject enlarges; all things sooner or later fall into place. As I am, so I see; use what language we will, we can never say anything but what we are; Hermes, Cadmus, Columbus, Newton, Bonaparte are the mind's ministers. Instead of feeling a poverty when we encounter a great man, let us treat the newcomer like a travelling geologist who passes through our estate and shows us good slate, or limestone, or anthracite, in our brush pasture. The partial ac-

tion of each strong mind in one direction is a telescope for the objects on which it is pointed. But every other part of knowledge is to be pushed to the same extravagance, ere the soul attains her due sphericity.

The blindness of the strong, Emerson implies, necessarily constitutes insight. Is the insight of the strong also blindness? Can a soul duly spherical be enough of an *unseeing* soul to go on writing poetry? Here is the gnomic poem that introduces *Experience*:

> The lords of life, the lords of life,—
> I saw them pass,
> In their own guise,
> Like and unlike,
> Portly and grim,
> Use and Surprise,
> Surface and Dream,
> Succession swift, and spectral Wrong,
> Temperament without a tongue,
> And the inventor of the game
> Omnipresent without name;—
> Some to see, some to be guessed,
> They marched from east to west:
> Little man, least of all,
> Among the legs of his guardians tall,
> Walked about with puzzled look.
> Him by the hand dear Nature took,
> Dearest Nature, strong and kind,
> Whispered, Darling, never mind!
> To-morrow they will wear another face,
> The founder thou! these are thy race!

This is the Emerson of about 1842, and if no longer a Primary, he is not quite a Secondary Man. The lords of life (and *Life* was the first title for *Experience*) are a rather dubious sevenfold to inspire any poet, and the more-than-Wordsworthian homely nurse, Nature, offers little comfort. If these are the gods, then man is sensible to be puzzled. But it all goes with a diabolically cheerful (though customarily awkward) lilt, and the indubitable prophet of our literary self-reliance seems as outrageously cheerful as ever. There aren't any good models in this procession, and man, Nature assures us, is *their* model, but we are urged to yet another mode of Self-Reliance anyway. "Ne te quaesiveris extra" (Do not seek yourself outside yourself), but what is it to seek yourself even within yourself? Does the essay *Experience*, in giving us, as I think it does, a vision beyond skepticism, give us also any way out of the double bind of poetic influence?

"We thrive by casualties," Emerson says, and while he means "random occurrences" he could as well have meant "losses." But these would have been casual losses, given up to "those who are powerful obliquely and not by the direct stroke." Very charmingly Emerson says of these masters that "one gets the cheer of their light without paying too great a tax." Such an influence Emerson himself hoped to be, but Thoreau and even Whitman paid a heavy tax for Emersonian light, and I suspect many contemporary Americans still pay something—whether or not they have read Emerson —since his peculiar relevance now is that we seem to read him merely by living here, in this place still somehow his, and not our own. His power over us attains an elevation in an astonishing recovery from skepticism that suddenly illuminates *Experience*:

> And we cannot say too little of our constitutional necessity of seeing things under private aspects. . . . And yet is the God the native of these bleak rocks. . . . We must hold hard to this poverty, ·however scandalous, and by more vigorous self-recoveries, after the sallies of action, possess our axis more firmly.

After this, Emerson is able to give us a blithe prose-list of "the lords of life": "Illusion, Temperament, Succession, Surface, Surprise, Reality, Subjectiveness"; and in accepting these he gives us also his escape from conflicting attitudes towards influence: "All I know is reception; I am and I have: but I do not get, and when I have fancied I had gotten anything, I found I did not." But there speaks the spheral man, the all-but-perfect solipsist who made Thoreau almost despair, and whom Whitman emulated only to end as a true poet in the grief-ridden palinode of "As I Ebbed with the Ocean of Life." Charles Ives, deeply under the influence of Emerson's late *Prudence*, movingly remarks: "Everyone should have the opportunity of not being over-influenced." Stevens, a less candid Emersonian, is far closer to *Experience* in his ecstatic momentary victories over influence:

> I have not but I am and as I am, I am.
> . . . .
> . . . Perhaps,
> The man-hero is not the exceptional monster,
> But he that of repetition is most master.

Emerson says: "I am and I have," because he receives without self-appropriation: "I do not get." Stevens says: "I have not but I am," because he does not receive, but appropriates for himself through mastering the repetition of his own never-ending meditation upon self. Emerson is the more perfect solipsist, and yet also the more generous spirit, thus getting the better of it both ways. Stevens, the better poet but the much less transcendent consciousness, is less persuasive in proclaiming an ultimate Self-Reliance. In this he does not differ, however, from all our Emersonian poets, whether voluntary like Whitman, Robinson, Frost, or involuntary like Dickinson and Melville. Stevens too, who saw himself as "A new scholar replacing an older one," became another involuntary ephebe of the Supreme Fiction of our literature, Emersonian individualism, which remains our most troublesome trope.

Recoiling from the consequences of an all-repellent individualism, Emerson opted first for Dionysiac influx and later for the dominance of that other Orphic presence, Ananke, who opposed herself to the individual as his own limitations perceived under the mark of a different aesthetic, the beauty of Fate. For Emerson's was an aesthetic of *use*, a properly pragmatic American aesthetic, which came to fear imaginative entropy as the worst foe of the adverting or questing mind seeking to make of its own utility of eloquence a vision of universal good.

What can be used can be used up; this is what Geoffrey Hartman calls "the anxiety of demand," a version of which is enacted in a fundamental Romantic genre, the crisis-lyric. Does the achieved poem give confidence that the next poem can be written? An Idealizing critic, even one of great accomplishment, evidently can believe that poets are concerned, as poets, only with the anxiety of form, and not at all with the anxieties of influence and of demand; but all form, however personalized, stems from influx, and all form, however depersonalized, shapes itself against depletion and so seeks to meet demand. Beneath the anxiety of demand is a ghost of all precursor-obsessions: the concern that inspiration may fail, whereas the strong illusion persists that inspiration could not fail the precursor, for did he not inspire the still-struggling poet?

Emerson's inspiration never failed, in part because it never wholly came to him, or if it did then it came mixed with considerable prudence, and generally arrived in the eloquence of prose. If the anxiety of influence descends as a myth of the father, then we can venture that the anxiety of demand is likely to manifest itself through concealing images of the mother or Muse. In Stevens, particularly in the late phase of *The Auroras of Autumn* and *The Rock*, the concealment is withdrawn:

> Farewell to an idea . . . The mother's face,
> The purpose of the poem, fills the room. . . .

But Stevens, for all his late bleakness, was preternaturally fecund, and did not suffer greatly from the anxiety of demand; nor did Emerson. Whitman did, and that sorrow still requires exploration by his readers. The anxiety induced by a vision of the imaginative father, however, is strongly Stevens', as here in the *Auroras:*

> The father sits
> In space, wherever he sits, of bleak regard,
>
> As one that is strong in the bushes of his eyes.
> He says no to no and yes to yes. He says yes
> To no; and in saying yes he says farewell.

This Jehovah-like affirmer, whose eyes have replaced the burning bush, is a composite figure, with Emerson and Whitman important components, since of all Stevens' precursors they most extravagantly said yes. The saying of farewell is equivocal. Stevens, more forcefully than Pound, exemplifies "making it new" through the freshness of transformation, and more comprehensively than Williams persuades us that the difficulties of cultural heritage cannot be overcome through evasions. Emerson, ancestor to all three, would have found in Stevens what he had once found in Whitman: a rightful heir of the American quest for a Self-Reliance founded upon a complete self-knowledge.

Contemporary American poetry, written in the large shadowings of Pound, Williams, Stevens and their immediate progeny, is an impossible heroic quest wholly in the Emersonian tradition, another variation on the native strain. The best of our contemporary poets show an astonishing energy of response to the sorrow of influence that forms so much of the hidden subject of their work. As heirs, sometimes unknowing, of Emerson, they receive also his heartening faith that "eloquence is the appropriate organ of the highest personal energy," and so they can participate also in the noblest of Emersonian conscious indulgences in the Optative Mood, the belief that influence, for a potentially strong poet, is only energy that comes from a precursor (as Emerson says) "of the same turn of mind as his own, and who sees much farther on his own way than he." On this Emersonian implicit theory of the imagination, literary energy is drawn from language and not from nature, and the influence-relationship takes place between words *and* words, and not between subjects. I am a little unhappy to find Emerson, even in one of his aspects, joining Nietzsche as a precursor of Jacques Derrida and Paul de Man, twin titans of deconstruction, and so I want to conclude this chapter by juxtaposing Derrida with Emerson on the anxiety of influence. First, Derrida:

> The concept of centered structure is in fact the concept of a freeplay based on a fundamental ground, a freeplay which is constituted upon a fundamental immobility and a reassuring certitude, which is itself beyond the reach of the freeplay. With this certitude anxiety can be mastered, for anxiety is invariably the result of a certain mode of being implicated in the game, of being caught by the game, of being as it were from the very beginning at stake in the game.

Against this, Emerson, from the essay *Nominalist and Realist*:

> For though gamesters say that the cards beat all the players, though they were never so skilful, yet in the contest we are now considering, the players are also the game, and share the power of the cards.

Nietzsche, according to Derrida, inaugurated the decentering that Freud, Heidegger, Lévi-Strauss and, most subversively, Derrida himself have accomplished in the Beulah-lands of Interpretation. Though I am myself an uneasy quester after lost meanings, I still conclude that I favor a kind of interpretation that seeks to restore and redress meaning, rather than primarily to deconstruct meaning. To de-idealize our vision of texts is a good, but a limited good, and I follow Emerson, as against Nietzsche, in declining to make of de-mystification the principal end of dialectical thought in criticism.

Marcuse, introducing Hegel yet sounding like a Kabbalist, insists that dialectical thinking must make the absent present "because the greater part of the truth is in that which is absent." Speech and "positive" thinking are false because they are "part of a mutilated whole." A Marxist dialectician like Adorno shows us clearly what dialectical thinking is in our time; the thinker self-consciously thinks about his thinking in the very act of intending the objects of his thought. Emerson, in *Nominalist and Realist*, still a genuinely startling text, simply says: "No sentence will hold the whole truth, and the only way in which we can be just, is by giving ourselves the lie. . . ." That is a wilder variety of dialectical thinking than most post-Hegelian Europeans attempt, and Emerson is in consequence as maddening as he is ingratiating. For, in Emerson, dialectical thought does not fulfill the primary function of fighting off the idealistic drive of an expanding consciousness. Both in his Transcendental and in his Necessitarian phases, Emerson doesn't worry about ending in solipsism; he is only too happy to reach the transparency of solipsism whenever he can. He is very much Wittgenstein's Schopenhauerian solipsist who knows he is right in what he *means*, and who knows also that he is in error in what he *says*. The solipsism of Emerson's Transcendentalism issues finally in the supra-realism of the Necessitarianism of his last great book, the magnificent *The Conduct of Life*. Dialectical thinking in Emerson does not attempt to bring us back to the world of things and of other selves, but only to a world of language, and so its purpose is never to *negate* what is directly before us. From a European perspective, probably, Emersonian thinking is not so much dialectical as it is plain crazy, and I suspect that even Blake would have judged Emerson to be asserting that "without negations there is no progression," a negation being for Blake opposed to a genuinely dialectical contrary. Yet Nietzsche, who could tolerate so few of his own contemporaries, delighted in Emerson, and seems to have understood Emerson very well. And I think Nietzsche particularly understood that Emerson had come to prophesy not a de-centering, as Nietzsche had, and as Derrida and de Man are brilliantly accomplishing, but a peculiarly American *re-centering*, and with it an American mode of interpretation, one that we have begun—but only begun— to develop, from Whitman and Peirce down to Stevens and Kenneth Burke; a mode that *is* intra-textual, but that stubbornly remains logocentric, and that still follows Emerson in valorizing eloquence, the inspired voice, *over* the scene of writing. Emerson, who said he unsettled all questions, first put literature into question for us, and now survives to question our questioners.

IO

In the shadow of Emerson

The philosophy we want is one of fluxions and mobility. . . .
We want a ship in these billows we inhabit. An angular, dog-
matic house would be rent to chips and splinters in this storm
of many elements. No, it must be tight, and fit to the form of
man, to live at all; as a shell must dictate the architecture of a
house founded on the sea. . . . *We are golden averages, voli-*
tant stabilities, compensated or periodic errors, houses founded
on the sea. . . .

Emerson, Montaigne; or The Skeptic

The central American poems are houses founded on the sea. This
chapter examines three representative post-Emersonian poems: *As I*
Ebb'd with the Ocean of Life, Because I could not stop for
Death—, The Auroras of Autumn, chosen because they are as
strong as any written by the strongest of our poets: Whitman,
Dickinson, Stevens. These poems and poets are Emersonian in a
double sense. They follow the seer in his insistence upon poetic
priority, the freshness of transformation, but also in his peculiar
dialectic of asking the poet to be at once wholly individual and
wholly part of the commonal. As ought by now to be clear, influ-
ence has little relation to overt attitudes. Whitman was a knowing
Emersonian and said so; Dickinson and Stevens read Emerson and
were equivocal in their knowing response, but their profound mis-
prision of him is essential to nearly everything they wrote.

Whitman barely displaces the English Romantic model of the

crisis-poem, nor does Stevens, who is despite appearances a profoundly Whitmanesque poet, rather more so than Hart Crane. Dickinson, who had her own antithetical struggle against the maleness of her central precursors, violently swerves from the model, yet its traces are strong in her. In all of these poets, starting from Emerson, there is an emphasis upon Sublime representation that seems peculiarly American. The daemonic is not uncanny to them. All excel at hyperbole, and all make more use of the defense of repression than any of their comparable British contemporaries, either in the nineteenth century or in ours.

Whitman is at once the greatest and the most repressed of American poets. If the surmise is correct that the poets invented all of the defenses, as well as all the tropes, then more is to be learned about why the repressed cannot wholly return by reading Whitman's *The Sleepers* than by reading Freud's essay "Repression." Freud thought that the repressed returns through a number of processes, but particularly through displacement, condensation and conversion. Whitman is a master of all three operations, but in him they converge, not to reverse repression, but to exalt repression into the American Sublime.

I choose *As I Ebb'd* because it is, to me, the most moving of all Whitman's poems, and if I am to justify an antithetical mode of practical criticism, even to myself, it must help me interpret such a poem. Here, as in my chapter on Milton's poetic descendants, I will try to remember that the common reader cares little to be taught to notice tropes or defenses. Images must suffice, and so I will concentrate on images, but will indicate the trope or the defense when it seems to me an inevitable aid to reading.

Emerson, Whitman's precursor, wrote the motto to Whitman's poem in his 1823 Journals: "The worst is, that the ebb is certain, long and frequent, while the flow comes transiently and seldom." A seer is always undoing himself, and only a few times mounts into the Sublime. Some remarks by Anna Freud in her book on defenses are relevant here:

The obscurity of a successful repression is only equalled by the transparency of the repressive process when the movement is reversed. . . .

Repression consists in the withholding or expulsion of an idea or affect from the conscious ego. It is meaningless to speak of repression where the ego is still merged with the id. . . .

The first of these remarks may help illuminate the constant emblem of the American Sublime down to Stevens: transparency. The second may remind us that the ephebe cannot mount up into the Sublime until he has separated himself, so far as he is capable of doing, from the internalized precursor. As we begin reading *As I Ebb'd*, with its rather complex opening irony, another of Anna Freud's observations is useful:

> . . . reaction-formation can best be studied when such formations are in process of disintegration. In such a case the id's inroad takes the form of a reinforcement of the libidinal cathexis of the primitive instinctual impulse which the reaction-formation concealed. This enables the impulse to force its way into consciousness and, for a time, the instinctual impulse and the reaction-formation are visible within the ego side by side. . . .

In terms of figuration, that is the same as saying one thing while meaning another, the *illusio* that in distintegrating itself allows a poem to begin. Once again, it hardly matters whether one calls a defense a concealed trope or a trope a concealed defense, for this kind of concealment *is* poetry.

Whitman's poem may be divided thus: section 1, *clinamen* and *tessera*; 2, *kenosis*; 3, *daemonization*; and 4, *askesis* and *apophrades*. That is, the first section moves from images of presence and absence to part/whole representations. The second section is a radical and regressive undoing, dominated by a large image of emptiness. With the third section, imagery of a fall into lowness dominates, in a beautifully grotesque version of sublimity. The fourth and last section juxtaposes an imagistic opposition of nature and Whit-

man's self as outside and inside with images of lateness accepted as such, and with the present firmly negated.

This application of the map of misreading is only a broad and rough one, for the entire poem is remarkable as a version of *kenosis*, of Whitman undoing the Whitmanian bardic self of *Song of Myself*. Yet it shows us how close Whitman is to the English Romantic crisis-poem, particularly to Shelley's *Ode to the West Wind*. For Shelley's leaves Whitman substitutes "those slender windrows,/ chaff, straw, splinters of wood, weeds" and the rest of his remarkable metonymic catalog. For Shelley's "trumpet of a prophecy," Whitman gives us "that blare of the cloud-trumpets," which helps give us a sense of glory as "we too lie in drifts" at the close of his poem.

Whitman's opening stanza, with its fierce swerve away from Emersonian Nature, is the poem in embryo:

> As I ebb'd with the ocean of life,
> As I wended the shores I know,
> As I walk'd where the ripples continually wash you Paumanok,
> Where they rustle up hoarse and sibilant,
> Where the fierce old mother endlessly cries for her castaways,
> I musing late in the autumn day, gazing off southward,
> Held by this electric self out of the pride of which I utter poems,
> Was seiz'd by the spirit that trails in the lines underfoot,
> The rim, the sediment that stands for all the water and all the land of the globe.

Like Shelley in a wood skirting the Arno, or Stevens confronting the auroras, Whitman muses "late in the autumn day." All three poems adopt a belated stance, with Whitman confronting the south, Shelley the west, and Stevens the north. Whitman gazes at Ferenczi's and tradition's emblem of the mother, Shelley at revolutionary change and death, Stevens at natural change and death. But Whitman, more powerfully than the others, gazes at poetic change and death also. His opening *illusio* or irony is the subtlest of the three. He says "I ebb'd" but he means that "this electric self"

ebbed, for it is the pride out of which he is able to write poems, the self of *Song of Myself*, that is ebbing. He is dying as a poet, he rightly fears. The fear is very close to the fear of Wordsworth, Shelley and Stevens, but the irony is more pervasive, since Whitman, following Emerson, proclaims a greater monism, yet Whitman is knowingly the most severely dualistic of these poets.

Yet Whitman moves to a restituting representation far more quickly than the others, in the overt synecdoche of "The rim, the sediment that stands for all the water and all the land of the globe." The beach for him is the greatest of synecdoches, standing for ocean and for earth, for mother and for father, but most of all for himself, Whitman, as human sufferer rather than as poet. The insight our map of misreading gives us here is precisely how the part/whole image of representation directly restitutes for the absence/presence image of limitation. Whitman walks the beach as man rather than as poet, "with that electric self seeking types" but not *as* that self. What the poem most quickly returns to him is the *tikkun* of being at once closer to both his father and his mother, whereas when most the poet he is farthest away from his father (as in *The Sleepers* and *Out of the Cradle Endlessly Rocking*).

The image of emptying out the self until it is only a windrow is already present in the first section, but totally dominates the second, where the defense of undoing the poetic self is more direct than anywhere else in the language, even in Shelley:

> I too but signify at the utmost a little wash'd-up drift,
> A few sands and dead leaves to gather,
> Gather, and merge myself as part of the sands and drift.

Beautiful as the first two sections are, they become dwarfed by the grandeur of the Sublime rising up so strangely and indeed in so American a way in the second half of the poem. Whitman's *daemonization* is a profound humanization of the Sublime, a repression that strengthens his life, that binds him more closely and savingly to earth:

I throw myself upon your breast my father,
I cling to you so that you cannot unloose me,
I hold you so firm till you answer me something.

Kiss me my father,
Touch me with your lips as I touch those I love,
Breathe to me while I hold you close the secret of the murmuring
    I envy.

Few writers reveal so well what repression truly defends against, and why repression is so close to the apotropaic function of representation, to the way in which poetry wards off destruction. What Whitman has repressed, *and goes on repressing*, now more strongly than ever, is the close association in him between the Primal Scene of Instruction (covenant with Emerson) and the Primal Scenes proper, Freud's *Urphantasie* and *Urszene* (refusal of covenant with Walter Whitman, Sr.). As the covenant with Emerson that begat the poetic self ebbs, so the rejected covenant with the actual father is accepted and made whole. Emersonian Self-Reliance freed Whitman from the totalizing afflictions of the family romance. Now the consequences of the poetic analogue of the family romance allow Whitman a reconciliation he never found while his father was alive. Imaginative loss quite literally is transformed into experiential gain, in a far more direct way than Wordsworth or Coleridge could have envisioned.

Original and life-enhancing as this is, Whitman goes beyond it in the magnificent final section of his poem. He begins with metaphor and its perspectives, yet goes beyond such dualism within six lines of his last section. The ocean of life or fierce old mother is outside him, but now she fears his touch more than he fears her, for he is one with the father. But the outside/inside relation of ocean-of-life/Whitman is too negative a knowledge to be long sustained. The astonishing last stanza of the poem is a grand scheme of transumption, troping again upon every crucial trope in the text preceding it:

Ebb, ocean of life, (the flow will return,)
Cease not your moaning you fierce old mother,
Endlessly cry for your castaways, but fear not, deny not me,
Rustle not up so hoarse and angry against my feet as I touch you
    or gather from you.

I mean tenderly by you and all,
I gather for myself and for this phantom looking down where we
    lead, and following me and mine.

Me and mine, loose windrows, little corpses,
Froth, snowy white, and bubbles,
(See, from my dead lips the ooze exuding at last,
See, the prismatic colors glistening and rolling,)
Tufts of straw, sands, fragments,
Buoy'd hither from many moods, one contradicting another,
From the storm, the long calm, the darkness, the swell,
Musing, pondering, a breath, a briny tear, a dab of liquid or soil,
Up just as much out of fathomless workings fermented and thrown,
A limp blossom or two, torn, just as much over waves floating,
    drifting at random,
Just as much for us that sobbing dirge of Nature,
Just as much whence we come that blare of the cloud-trumpets,
We, capricious, brought hither we know not whence, spread out
    before you,
You up there walking or sitting,
Whoever you are, we too lie in drifts at your feet.

The "just as much" repetition is the agency by which the metonymy of "Me and mine, loose windrows, little corpses" becomes the metalepsis of "We, capricious, brought hither we know not whence." As a metonymy of a metonymy, the "We, capricious" triumphantly reverses the reductive pattern of the poem, for the present time in which Whitman is cut off from his poetic self becomes a wholly negated time, and so no time at all. The poetic past is introjected, and the images of lateness become exalted:

Just as much for us that sobbing dirge of Nature
Just as much whence we come that blare of the cloud-trumpets. . . .

If we put this in terms of the transformation of defenses, we would say that undoing has been undone by introjection, that the self has come to a rest in an identification with an earlier version of what once it was (or fantasizes itself to have been). But I would prefer to call this finally a strong or deep misreading of Emerson's *Nature*, in its apocalyptic conclusion:

> Know then that the world exists for you. For you is the phenomenon perfect. What we are, that only can we see. . . . Build therefore your own world. . . . The kingdom of man over nature, which cometh not with observation,—a dominion such as now is beyond his dream of God,—he shall enter without more wonder than the blind man feels who is gradually restored to perfect sight.

From Emerson's "for you" to Whitman's "just as much for us" is a long movement, when "for us" means "me and mine, loose windrows" and not the spirit made a giant through influx. Whitman's ultimate misprision of the seer his master is to assert that the blind man is restored to sight by the ebb, rather than the flow.

Dickinson's argument with Emerson is even more intimate, as she was a perpetual heretic whose only true orthodoxy was Emersonianism, or the exaltation of whim. Her stance is rarely belated, because of her exquisite good fortune in having only precursors who were merely male—even Emerson, for all his universalism. Her argument with Emerson turns on and against his iron law of Compensation, which for her was not iron enough. "Nothing is got for nothing," he keeps saying, in his cheerfully daemonic way, and her reply is "Nothing is got for everything," though her "nothing" is rather larger than every subsequent poet's "everything." What can our map of misreading do to or for her, or does her originality extend so far that she passes beyond our revisionary model?

Often she does, but not I think in her most famous and now most favored poems, for these do tend to follow the traditional model. I will use no. 712, *Because I could not stop for Death—*, for its fame, but also for its poetic power. This six-stanza poem divides into our triadic structure with some revealing emphases. The first stanza moves from irony to synecdoche. The next three stanzas proceed from an emptying-out of the self and things, to an hyperbolic transcending of nature. In the poem's fifth stanza, metaphor mysteriously presents itself and fails, to be replaced in the final stanza by a metaleptic reversal that tropes triumphantly upon time.

Dickinson's opening trope plays on a social convention and on two meanings of "stop": Miss Dickinson of Amherst, despite her regard for him, cannot make a public call upon Death. Death, as a New England gentleman, shows his civility by calling upon her in his carriage. But also, rather like Shelley, Miss Dickinson always goes on until she is stopped, and she never is stopped, even by or for death. Yet Dickinson the poet clearly says one thing and means another. She means that Death cannot arrest her consciousness, but she can and does his, which is a rather complex irony. The reader is likely still to be struggling with her wit at condensation, when he has to take on her answering synecdoche: the carriage holds Death and the lady, but also her chaperone or duenna, Immortality.

Death then is more than overmatched, and this in but one stanza! Yet his civility limits the gentlewoman, and in exchange she has isolated herself, from labor and from leisure. This *kenosis* is extended through regression by the image of children at play, and through undoing by the pathetic fallacy of the "Gazing Grain." Yet no self-limitation abides long in the formidable Dickinson, and her *daemonization* into a personal version of the American Sublime is as sudden as it is original, and as powerfully repressive as Whitman's or Nietzsche's solar trajectories:

We passed the Setting Sun—

Or rather—He passed Us—
The Dews drew quivering and chill—
For only Gossamer, my Gown—
My Tippet—only Tulle—

Dressed presumably for an afternoon drive, she has joined some system or body greater than the sun, about which the sun revolves, and yet still enough of earth to chill her with evening dews. As Sublime representation, a hyperbole cast beyond the sun, this conceals (barely) a defense against the largest of desires for a poet, poetic immortality. The duenna who rides with Dickinson cannot be faith and must be her own poetry, and since a woman poet reduces the male to muse, Death is put in his perfectly civil place, as Dickinson's muse, dangerous enough but unable to consummate his desire (which is also her desire—he stopped for her because she *could* not socially, rather than would not).

With the fifth stanza, the failed perspectivism of *askesis* is again upon us, but Dickinson fails knowingly and gloriously:

> We paused before a House that seemed
> A Swelling of the Ground—
> The Roof was scarcely visible—
> The Cornice—in the Ground—

It isn't possible to call either the House or the Ground inside or outside, and if the metaphor substitutes for Dickinson's tomb (I do not think it does) then it contradicts itself into incoherence. But I read the stanza as meaning that in the vision she has entered, all perspective is abolished, which in terms of defense means that no sublimation of desire, any desire, is possible any longer. But again she will not let her reader pause; she removes herself from time, and time from her reader. Our belatedness is our earliness. She has ridden with Death (and Immortality) for centuries, yet it is less than the Day of her first self-recognition, her first apprehension that the chariot belonged to her own poetry.

A gnomic poet calls for a gnomic commentary; the seer of *The Auroras of Autumn* demands considerable discursiveness. His poem calls for its own version of the map of misreading, in which the roman numerals refer to the ten sections or cantos of the poem, and the dominating images are identified:

Clinamen I Serpent as presence and absence.

Tessera II-IV Farewell to an idea as synecdoche of a farewell to all of life, through the part-image of a farewell to poetry.

Kenosis V Metonymy of barbarous tongue and breath; emptying-out of festival image.

Daemonization VI American Sublime, theatre of hyperbole; skyscape as image of the high, scholar of one candle as image of the low.

Askesis VII Diamond crown cabala as failed metaphor; sublimation into flippant communication under the moon.

Apophrades VIII-X Time of innocence as transumptive reversal; introjection of auroras, projection of death.

The simple irony of Stevens' opening canto is that he says change but means death, which is the double meaning of the serpent who is at once a total presence and a total absence:

This is form gulping after formlessness,
Skin flashing to wished-for disappearances
And the serpent body flashing without the skin.

Perry Miller, who traced the progression from Jonathan Edwards to Emerson, provides an excellent motto for *The Auroras of Autumn* in his study of the New England mind in the seventeenth century:

There must be room in the universe for a free and unpredictable power, for a lawless force that flashes through the night in unexpected brilliance and unaccountable majesty. It was better in Puritan eyes that most men be passed over by this illumination and left to hopeless despair rather than that all men should be born without the hope of beholding it, or that a few should forgo the ecstasy of the vision.

As Emerson displaced this sense of election, so Stevens, a new scholar replacing an older one, freshly transformed election into what he called imagination. But the price is what Stevens comes to at last in *The Auroras of Autumn,* where as fundamentalist of his own First Idea he confronts the free and unpredictable force of the Northern Lights, which do not consent to be reduced.

The Lurianic dialectic that I have displaced into Limitation → Substitution → Representation is in Stevens wholly explicit. The three stages in him are called: Reduction to the First Idea → Being Unable to Live with the First Idea alone → Re-imagining the First Idea. Cantos II-IV of the *Auroras* show Stevens moving from a reaction-formation against his own fears of impotence and death into a turning-against-the-self that he calls "Farewell to an idea . . . ," where the idea is not so much the First Idea as it is the whole triple process that has been the dialectic of Stevens' perception, and so of his thought and his poetry. Poetry stands here for all of life, so that the synecdoche is very dark:

> Here, being visible is being white,
> Is being of the solid of white, the accomplishment
> Of an extremist in an exercise . . .
>
> The season changes. A cold wind chills the beach.
> The long lines of it grow longer, emptier,
> A darkness gathers though it does not fall
>
> And the whiteness grows less vivid on the wall.

The extremist is Stevens, the exercise is reduction to the First Idea, the accomplishment is the beach-world, intolerable because it has been reduced wholly from the nothing that is not there to the nothing that is. The First Idea is a perception stripped of the Pathetic Fallacy, an object-world wholly object, with no illusion and with no humanity. Yet the intended function of the First Idea was that it should be "the quick / Of this invention," where the invention was "this invented world" of *Notes Toward a Supreme Fiction.* What there was called "that ever-early candor," a white origin of poetic sincerity and truth, has become now the poisonous "solid of white" that is the colorless all-color of the aging Stevens' stricken and perhaps dying imagination.

As I give here only the outline of a reading, I will neglect the beauties of cantos II-IV, where successively the cabin (Emerson's "house founded on the sea"), the *imago* of the mother ("The soft hands are a motion not a touch") and of the father ("in saying yes he says farewell") are all reduced to the failed First Idea. In canto V, these dismissed images are brought together only to be undone, in one large image that is emptied out of all significance:

> We stand in the tumult of a festival.
> What festival? This loud, disordered mooch?

The father's images of theatre are those of metonymy: "his unherded herds, / Of barbarous tongue, slavered and panting halves / Of breath." Everything that rejoices is undone, or carried back through a regression that cannot sustain its own nostalgia: "The children laugh and jangle a tinny time." This limitation is so extreme in its images, even for Stevens, that the reaction of *daemonization*, into an American Sublime, becomes the most violent and sustained hyperbole in all of Stevens. Images of height mount to a theatre of skyscape, that cannot be qualified even by Stevens' characteristic defensive irony:

> Splashed wide-wise because it likes magnificence
> And the solemn pleasures of magnificent space.

When the theatre collapses, as it must, Stevens achieves the apotheosis of his own repression, in the single passage that moves me most in all his work:

> This is nothing until in a single man contained,
> Nothing until this named thing nameless is
> And is destroyed. He opens the door of his house

On flames. The scholar of one candle sees
An Arctic effulgence flaring on the frame
Of everything he is. And he feels afraid.

Dickinson would have admired this, since it counts the cost of an American Sublime almost as tellingly as she did. Stevens attempts again, for a last time, to repeat the discipline of his poetry in the face of the auroras, but he cannot un-name the Northern Lights. Lingering in his mind are earlier triumphs when he had the power to destroy named things:

Throw away the lights, the definitions,
And say of what you see in the dark

That it is this or that it is that,
But do not use the rotted names.

       *   *   *

There is a project for the sun. The sun
Must bear no name, gold flourisher, but be
In the difficulty of what it is to be.

But *these* lights will not be thrown away, and there is no project for the auroras. Stevens' house founded on the sea opens on flames, and the height to which the highest candle lights the dark proves not to be very high. From this hyperbole that has failed, not as representation, but as argument, Stevens attempts the final limitation of his characteristic *askesis*, in the sublimating metaphor of canto VII.

This canto returns to (or continues in) skyscape, but this is a very different sky, dominated by a mortal god, an Ananke or Beautiful Necessity (Emerson's term, in *The Conduct of Life*) whose imagination sits enthroned in the constellations, descending to extinguish our planets, when it will:

Leaving, of where we were and looked, of where

We knew each other and of each other thought,
A shivering residue, chilled and foregone,
Except for that crown and mystical cabala.

This crown and mystical or diamond cabala (did Stevens know the word originally meant "reception"?) is the extended metaphor by which the poet hopes finally to make peace with the auroras, as a Platonic-Emersonian deity that demands and deserves worship, because it is beautiful and because the extinction of the poet's answering violence-of-the-mind thus becomes part of the necessity of this violence-of-the-sky. But Stevens, like Dickinson, cannot accept metaphor, with its subject-object distinctions penning the poet's mind in self-contradiction. For even the aurora, crown and mystical cabala of the heavens, "dare not leap by chance in its own dark." Like Shelley before him, Stevens is a Lucretian, and finds his image of freedom in the *clinamen* or swerve: "It must change from destiny to slight caprice." Sublimating his own metaphor, Stevens makes of the auroras another earthly poet, bound by the necessities or the pragmatics of human communication. The auroras-as-crown "move to find / What must unmake it," which can be no more than "Say, a flippant communication under the moon."

What follows is one of Stevens' finest inventions, a return of transumptive allusion so dazzling as to suggest Stevens as being a kind of minor Milton of our century. Cantos VIII-X conclude the poem with a full-scale reversal of early for late, centering on the image of a time of innocence. Introjecting the auroras, and projecting death away from him, for a brief time anyway, Stevens identifies himself with what earlier had terrified him:

> So, then, these lights are not a spell of light,
> A saying out of a cloud, but innocence.
> An innocence of the earth and no false sign
>
> Or symbol of malice. . . .

Stevens combines Keats and Whitman, and accomplishes a transumption of them both. The last three cantos argue an innocence of which Stevens can affirm: "Its nature is its end" and bring back the comforting mother of *Song of Myself*. "The idiom of an innocent earth" allows the skyscape to flash "Like a great shadow's last embellishment," and restores a Whitmanian sense of a maternal death:

> It may come tomorrow in the simplest word,
> Almost as part of innocence, almost,
> Almost as the tenderest and the truest part.

The price, as always in transumption, is the reality of the present moment, vanished between a lateness made early again, and a lost earliness now seen as belated. "By these lights," the auroras, Stevens might know, but only "Like a blaze of summer straw, in winter's nick"; and he does not tell us what it is that he might know.

II

In the shadow of the shadows: for now

I have been tracing the visionary company that inhabits two shadows of influence, the Miltonic tradition that goes from the poets of Sensibility to its culmination in Yeats, and the Emersonian tradition from Whitman to its completion in the last phase of Stevens. This final chapter, a brief speculation on contemporary poetry, will center on interpretative problems presented by what seems to me a revival of the transumptive mode in recent American verse, notably a significant late phase of Robert Penn Warren's work and extensions of the current phases of John Ashbery and A. R. Ammons.

Stevens' revival of transumptive allusion, as opposed to the conspicuous allusion of Pound, Eliot and their school, has its parallel in Warren's recent work, despite Warren's descent from the rival school of Eliot. Warren's *Audubon: A Vision*, like his work in progress, confirms the development over forty years of another strong poet to take the place left vacant by the deaths of the major American poets of this century. In his sixties, Warren has become the major contemporary revisionist of the native strain in American poetry. This is one of his recent poems, *Sunset Walk in Thaw-Time in Vermont*:

1

Rip, whoosh, wing-whistle: and out of
The spruce thicket, beating the snow from
Black spruce boughs, it

Bursts. The great partridge cock, black against flame-red,
Into the red sun of sunset, plunges. Is
Gone.

In the ensuing
Silence, abrupt in
Back-flash and shiver of that sharp startlement, I
Stand. Stare. In mud-streaked snow,
My feet are. I,
Eyes fixed past black spruce boughs on the red west, hear,
In my chest, as from a dark cave of
No-Time, the heart
Beat.

Where
Have the years gone?

2

All day the stream, thaw-flooding, foamed down its gorge.
Now, skyless but for the high-tangled spruce night, it
Moves, and the bulge and slick twining of muscular water, foam-
Slashed and white-tettered, glints now only in
The cold, self-generating light of snow
Strong yet in the darkness of rock-banks.

The boulder
Groans in the stream, the stream heaves
In the deep certainty of its joy, like
Doom, and I,
Eyes fixed yet on the red west, begin to hear—though
Slow and numb as upon waking—
The sound of water that moves in darkness.

I stand, and in my imagination see
The slick heave of water, blacker than basalt, and on it
The stern glint, like steel, of snow-darkness.

3

On the same spot in summer, at thrush-hour, I
As the last light fails, have heard that full
Shadow-shimmered and deep-glinting liquidity, and
Again will; but not now.

Now
Here stare westward, and hear only

The movement of darkening water, and from
Whatever depth of being I am, ask
To be made worthy of my human failure and folly, and
Worthy of my human ignorance and anguish, and of
What soul-stillness may be achieved as I
Stand here with the cold exhalation of snow
Coiling high as my knees.
                          Meanwhile,
On the mountain's east hump, darkness coagulates, and
Already, where sun has not touched for hours, the new
Ice-crystal frames its massive geometry.

4

When my son is an old man, and I have not,
For some fifty years, seen his face, and, if seeing it,
Would not even be able to guess what name it wore, what
Blessing should I ask for him?

That some time, in thaw-season, at dusk, standing
At woodside and staring
Red-westward, with the sound of moving water
In his ears, he
Should thus, in that future moment, bless,
Forward into that future's future,
An old man who, as he is mine, had once
Been his son.

For what blessing may a man hope for but
An immortality in
The loving vigilance of death?

If we apply to Warren's moving sequence our typology of eva-
sions, it falls into three divisions, sections 1, 2, and 3-4. Section 1
begins with an extraordinary *clinamen*, tracing the almost instan-
taneous movement of the partridge cock from overwhelming pres-
ence to total absence. The trope of irony here performs a double
labor, for the bird's disappearance into the sunset is what makes
this sunset visible to Warren, by clearing the spruce boughs. With
the bird's burst of appearance, like an origin or sunrise, comes no
time of apprehension of origins, but only the back-flash of Warren's

startlement, one of the most eloquent of his obsessive visions of time and of the immediacy of his own mortality. As a reaction-formation against his instinctual passion for death, Warren's breath-soul, the relation between his rhythm and diction, yields to an extreme rigidity, a cramping of a fierceness of spirit endemic in this poet. The answering representation, the reversal that is a synec-doche, is in the open question "Where /Have the years gone?" which is the whole completing the part that is the sudden end of a day in thaw-time. Compare this with the opening sections of *The Auroras of Autumn*, a poem in the Emersonian tradition that War-ren has sought to overturn. Stevens characteristically learns absence by too-abundant a presence, the violent beauty of the auroras. Warren, staring at the red west, is absence confronting absence, a child of Melville and Hawthorne rather than of Emerson and Whitman. The direct precursor for Warren is Eliot, but few con-temporary poets know so well as Warren the strength of all rele-vant tradition.

With section 2 we have Warren's *kenosis*, his metonymic undo-ing of his own vision. Isolation rather than regression is Warren's mode of emptying-out the poetic self. Where in section 1 he could hear his heart beat, now he hears the metonymic personifications of a sensibility momentarily deranged by startlement. Boulder and stream are fallen consciousnesses, and Warren is close to them, to sleep and death, as he begins to hear "the sound of water that moves in darkness." The movement from reductive hearing to hyperbolical sight in the section's closing triad is the answer of Warren's *daemonization*, his mounting into the American Counter-Sublime. In section 3, the imagery of high and low is blended with a perspectivism that achieves a Dantesque sense of terror, trans-forming the Emersonian-Stevensian transparency of crystal into something closer to the crystal of Revelation:

> Meanwhile,
> On the mountain's east hump, darkness coagulates, and
> Already, where sun has not touched for hours, the new
> Ice-crystal frames its massive geometry.

This is Warren's *askesis*, his sublimation through metaphor of personal death into impersonal meaningfulness, the "massive geometry" of the ice-crystal. Since the poem meditates continually on the contrasts implied by sunset and thaw-time, the crystal's geometry is the reconciliation such meditation intends, the point of perspective where nature, as outside, and Warren's intimations of mortality, as inside, are brought together. The metaphor "fails" in the peculiar sense I indicated in Chapter 5, that is, through the failure of perspectivism to redress a poetic crisis of meaning by a restitution of meaning.

Warren's originality and power, strong throughout the poem, is strongest in section 4, a transumption without rival in American poetry since *The Auroras of Autumn*. In a proleptic representation, Warren has a vision timed half a century after his own death, yielding all possible recognition to the necessity and force of change. His blessing for his son at once doubly introjects the future and projects all the past, annihilating the "red-westward" of the poem's present moment. By blessing "forward into the future's future," Warren manifests an *amor fati* akin to Nietzsche's or such Nietzschean followers as Yeats and Mann. At seventy-four, finishing *The Holy Sinner* (1951), Mann wrote of his work what Warren could say of his own late version of the proleptic blessing:

> AMOR FATI—I have little against being a late comer, one of the last, a finisher, and I do not believe that this story and the Joseph stories will ever be told again after me. . . .

Wordsworth blessing his sister at the conclusion of *Tintern Abbey*, and Coleridge in many similar moments, are the ultimate ancestors of Warren's poem, which may not be written again after him. "Immortality in / The loving vigilance of death" relies for its meaning on a transcending of "vigilance," through resort to its root meaning of "alertness." Warren, pugnaciously anti-Emersonian, reaches the freshness of transformation with a conscious belatedness that yet revives the Emersonian refusal to be late.

In turning to Ammons and Ashbery, criticism finds the Emersonian tradition becoming both the immediate burden and the immediate strength, whether of these poets or of their interpreters. To talk about a poem by Ammons or Ashbery in terms of Emerson or Whitman or Stevens is to invoke what one might term the Human Analogue, as opposed to Coleridge's Organic Analogue. No poem rejoices in its own solitary inscape, any more than we can do so. We have to be talked about in terms of other people; for no more than a poem can we be "about" ourselves. To say that a poem is about itself is killing, but to say it is about another poem is to go out into the world where we live. We idealize ourselves when we isolate ourselves, just as poets deceive themselves by idealizing what they assert to be their poems' true subjects. The actual subjects move towards the anxiety of influence, and now frequently are that anxiety. But a deeper apparent digression begins to loom here, even as I attempt to relate the peripheries and saliences of Ammons and the random epiphanies of Ashbery to the great circumferences and more central privileged moments of their transcendental ancestors.

Reductively, the anxiety of influence *is* the fear of death, and a poet's vision of the vigilance of immortality includes a freedom from influence. Sexual jealousy is a closely related anxiety in common experience and also reduces to the fear of death, or the ultimate tyranny of time and space as a dungeon, as the danger of domination by the Not-Me (which, as Emerson said, includes one's own body). Anxiety of influence, like jealousy, is due partly to fear of the natural body, yet poetry is written by the natural man who is one with the body. Blake insisted that there was also the "Real Man the Imagination." Perhaps there is, but he cannot write poems, at least not yet.

The poem attempts to relieve the poet-as-poet from fears that *there is not enough for him*, whether of imaginative space or in the priority of time. A subject, a mode, a voice; all these lead to the question: "What, besides my death, is my own?" Contemporary verse-writers of the various Pound-Williams schools scoff at the notion of an anxiety of influence, believing as they think they do that a poem is a machine made out of words. Perhaps, but mostly in the sense that we, alas, appear to be machines made out of words. Men make poems as Dr. Frankenstein made his *daimon*, and poems too acquire the disorders of the human. The people in poems do not have fathers, but the poems do.

Ammons and Ashbery, like Warren, are aware of all this, for strong poets become strong by meeting the anxiety of influence, not by ignoring it. Poets adept at forgetting their ancestry write very forgettable poems. They want to believe, with Nietzsche, that "forgetfulness is a property of all action," and action for them can only be writing a poem. But no poet can write a poem without, in some sense, remembering another poem, even as no one loves without remembering, however dimly, a former beloved, however fantasized or however much that came under a taboo. Every poet is forced to say, as Hart Crane did in an early poem: "I can remember much forgetfulness." To continue as a poet, a poet needs the illusive mist about him that shields him from the light that first kindled him. This mist is the nimbus (however falsely seen) of what the prophets would have called his own *kabod*, the supposed radiance of his own glory.

These ought to be obvious truths, but poets, supposedly defending poetry, idealize their relation to one another, and the magical Idealists among critics follow the poets in this self-deception. Northrop Frye idealizes more powerfully than even Blake does, in this regard:

> Once the artist thinks in terms of influence rather than of clarity of form, the effort of the imagination becomes an effort of will, and art is perverted into tyranny, the application of the principle of magic or mysterious compulsion to society.

Against this I cite Coleridge's remark that the power of originating *is* the will, our means of escaping from nature or repetition-compulsion; and I add that no one needs to pervert art in this respect, since the Post-Enlightenment poetic imagination is necessarily quite perverse enough in the perpetual battle against influence. Frye states the ideal; Coleridge knew we must make, as he said, "a *clinamen* to the ideal." As I now realize, Coleridge in his *Aids to Reflection* inaugurated the critical concept of what he called the "*lene clinamen,* the gentle bias," which I mistakenly thought I had invented for myself. Critics also are gifted at vain forgetfulness.

Ammons has suggested that the anxiety of influence "is part of the larger subject of hierarchy," a subject he sees as centered, for poets and critics, on the processes of canon-formation, which is ultimately a society's choices of texts for perpetuation and study. Canon-formation is not an arbitrary process, and is not, for more than a generation or two, socially or politically determined, even by the most intense of literary politics. Poets survive because of inherent strength; this strength is manifested through their influence upon other strong poets, and influence that goes through more than two generations of strong poets tends to become part of tradition, even to become the tradition itself. Poems stay alive when they engender live poems, even through resistance, resentment, misinterpretation; and poems become immortal when their descendants in turn engender vital poems. Out of the strong comes forth strength, even if not sweetness, and when strength has imposed itself long enough, then we learn to call it tradition, whether we like it or not.

Ammons and Ashbery, though the struggle for survival necessarily becomes more and more difficult, are probable candidates for survival, as is the later Warren. As a text from recent Ammons, I cite the dedicatory lines to his long poem, *Sphere: The Form of a Motion:*

> I went to the summit and stood in the high nakedness:
> the wind tore about this

way and that in confusion and its speech could not
get through to me nor could I address it:
still I said as if to the alien in myself
    I do not speak to the wind now:
for having been brought this far by nature I have been
brought out of nature
and nothing here shows me the image of myself:
for the word *tree* I have been shown a tree
and for the word *rock* I have been shown a rock,
for stream, for cloud, for star
this place has provided firm implication and answering
    but where here is the image for *longing*:
so I touched the rocks, their interesting crusts:
I flaked the bark of stunt-fir:
I looked into space and into the sun
and nothing answered my word *longing*:
    goodbye, I said, goodbye, nature so grand and
reticent, your tongues are healed up into their own
element
and as you have shut up you have shut me out: I am
as foreign here as if I had landed, a visitor:
so I went back down and gathered mud
and with my hands made an image for *longing*:
    I took the image to the summit: first
I set it here, on the top rock, but it completed
nothing: then I set it there among the tiny firs
but it would not fit:
so I returned to the city and built a house to set
the image in
and men came into my house and said
    that is an image for *longing*
and nothing will ever be the same again

In Chapter 5, I referred to different poetic structures as depart-
ing from the crisis-poem model by different applications of the
principle of rhetorical substitution, including a kind of poem that
begins in Sublime hyperbole, undoes itself metonymically, and then
moves through the opposition between metalepsis and metaphor to
end in an oscillation between synecdoche and irony. In each in-

stance, the representation is undone by the limitation, which is the pattern Ammons sets for himself here. His last line, despite his deepest impulses, is an irony or reaction-formation, proclaiming absence but actually acknowledging the continued presence of the need that first drove him into poetry, which is a need for the tongues of nature. His goodbye to nature is akin to Stevens' *Farewell to Florida*, for whenever Stevens says "hated" he means "loved," and whenever Ammons says "goodbye" he means "begin again."

On this reading, the last line of *I Went to the Summit* means that nothing in longing can change, or that the transcendental impulse cannot be ended (Emerson: "I am *Defeated* all the time; yet to Victory I am born"). The image of the house is the Emersonian synecdoche from *Nature* that Stevens had to employ in the crisis of *The Auroras of Autumn* when as American "scholar of one candle" he discovered he could not un-name the auroras: "He opens the door of his house / On flames." Ammons is much closer to Emerson, uncannily so, as Frost was; and like Frost he renews the implicit chill that Emerson's rhapsodies do not dispel. "Every spirit builds itself a house, and beyond its house a world, and beyond its world a heaven," and yet Emerson's major synecdoche tells us that we are ruins, mocked by the houses and worlds and heavens that we build:

> Man is the dwarf of himself. Once he was permeated and dissolved by spirit. He filled nature with his overflowing currents. . . . But, having made for himself this huge shell, his waters retired; he no longer fills the veins and veinlets; he is shrunk to a drop. He sees that the structure still fits him, but fits him colossally. Say, rather, once it fitted him, now it corresponds to him from far and on high. He adores timidly his own work. . . . Yet sometimes he starts in his slumber, and wonders at himself and muses strangely at the resemblance betwixt him and it. . . .

Ammons muses strangely at his resemblance to his own poetry, but psychically the trope is a defensive reversal, so that the image for *longing* is a fearful self-recognition, which is that Ammons will never again come to Unity, to the influx of Newness violently celebrated in his own earliest poetry. "The worst is, that the ebb is certain, long and frequent, while the flow comes transiently and seldom," Emerson wrote in his 1823 Journal, but the very worst is that it never comes again. That is the burden of the middle part of Ammons' poem, where he knows his own belatedness (here called being "foreign" or "shut out") and fails to reverse it by the metaphor of fashioning the mud-image of *longing*. To long is to desire while knowing that desire never can be fulfilled, or metaphorically here it is to see that the image, even if it filled all space, could not suffice.

This poem's greatness is partly in the audacity of its Sublime opening, where it is nature (the wind) that is "in confusion" and not the unspent seer; but more in the strength of the seer's metonymic undoings. If it is, as Emerson prophesied, the use of life to learn metonymy, Ammons demands more of life than such a use, while declining to dispute his precursor: "and nothing here shows me the image of myself." As with Warren's poem on the thaw-time sunset, a reader can be powerfully moved and even (momentarily) transformed by Ammons' high chant, yet still wonder if this strength of conscious belatedness does not work so as to close out yet another mode of poetry.

I close this chapter, and this book, with a haunting lyric of belatedness, John Ashbery's recent *As You Came from the Holy Land*, where the parodistic first-line/title repeats the opening of a bitter ballad of lost love attributed to Ralegh, one of whose stanzas lingers throughout Ashbery's gentler poem:

> I have lovde her all my youth,
>   Butt now ould, as you see,
> Love lykes not the fallyng frute
>   From the wythered tree.

"Her" is the personal past in Ashbery's elegy for the self:

AS YOU CAME FROM THE HOLY LAND

of western New York state
were the graves all right in their bushings
was there a note of panic in the late August air
because the old man had peed in his pants again
was there turning away from the late afternoon glare
as though it too could be wished away
was any of this present
and how could this be
the magic solution to what you are in now
whatever has held you motionless
like this so long through the dark season
until now the women come out in navy blue
and the worms come out of the compost to die
it is the end of any season

you reading there so accurately
sitting not wanting to be disturbed
as you came from that holy land
what other signs of earth's dependency were upon you
what fixed sign at the crossroads
what lethargy in the avenues
where all is said in a whisper
what tone of voice among the hedges
what tone under the apple trees
the numbered land stretches away
and your house is built in tomorrow
but surely not before the examination
of what is right and will befall
not before the census
and the writing down of names

remember you are free to wander away
as from other times other scenes that were taking place
the history of someone who came too late
the time is ripe now and the adage
is hatching as the seasons change and tremble
it is finally as though that thing of monstrous interest
were happening in the sky
but the sun is setting and prevents you from seeing it

out of night the token emerges
its leaves like birds alighting all at once under a tree
taken up and shaken again
put down in weak rage
knowing as the brain does it can never come about
not here not yesterday in the past
only in the gap of today filling itself
as emptiness is distributed
in the idea of what time it is
when that time is already past

Ashbery, probably because of his direct descent from Stevens, tends like Stevens to follow rather precisely the crisis-poem paradigm that I have traced in my map of misreading. This model, Wordsworthian-Whitmanian, never restores as much representational meaning as it continually curtails or withdraws, as I have observed earlier. Ashbery's resource has been to make a music of the poignance of withdrawal. So, in this poem, the "end of any season" that concludes the first stanza is deliberately too partial a synecdoche to compensate for the pervasive absences of the ironies throughout the stanza. Ashbery's turnings-against-the-self are wistful and inconclusive, and he rarely allows a psychic reversal any completeness. His origins, in the holy land of western New York state, are presented here and elsewhere in his work with an incurious rigidity that seems to have no particular design on the poet himself, characteristically addressed as "you." The next stanza emphasizes Ashbery's usual metonymic defense of isolation (as opposed to the Stevensian undoing or the Whitmanian regression), by which signs and impulses become detached from one another, with the catalog or census completing itself in the reductive "writing down of names," in which "down" takes on surprising difference and force. The third stanza, one of Ashbery's most radiant, marks the poem's *daemonization*, the American Counter-Sublime in which Ashbery, like Stevens, is so extraordinarily at home. Ashbery's mingled strength and weakness, indeed his deliberate pathos, is that he knowingly begins where Childe Roland ended, "free to wander away" yet always seeing himself as living "the history of someone who came too late" while sensing that "the time is ripe now." Studying his own habitual expression in his prose *Three Poems*, he had compared himself explicitly to Childe Roland at the Dark Tower. Here also, his Sublime sense that a Stevensian reality is happening in the war of the sky against the mind is necessarily obscured by a sunset akin to Roland's "last red leer."

Ashbery's finest achievement, to date, is his heroic and perpetual self-defeat, which is of a kind appropriate to conclude this book, since such self-defeat pioneers in undoing the mode of transumption that Stevens helped revive. Ashbery's allusiveness is transumptive rather than conspicuous, but he employs it against itself, as though determined to make of his lateness a desperate cheerfulness. In the final stanza of *As You Came from the Holy Land*, the most characteristic of Shelleyan-Stevensian metaphors, the fiction of the leaves, is duly revealed as a failure ("taken up and shaken again / put down in weak rage"); but the metalepsis substituted for it is almost a hyperbole of failure, as presence and the present fall together "in the gap of today filling itself / as emptiness is distributed." The two lines ending the poem would be an outrageous parody of the transumptive mode if their sad dignity were not so intense. Ashbery, too noble and poetically intelligent to subside into a parodist of time's revenges, flickers on "like a great shadow's last embellishment."